Rape of the Wild

Andrée Collard was born in Brussels in 1926 and emigrated to America in 1945. She was awarded an M.A. in Romance Literature from the National University of Mexico in 1955 and a Ph.D. in the same field from Harvard in 1964. Associate Professor of Romance and Comparative Literature at Brandeis University, Waltham, Massachusetts, until 1986, she also taught Women's Studies, having helped to establish the program in 1971-73. She was considered an authority on the Spanish Baroque for her study *Nueva Poesía: Conceptismo, Culteranismo en la Critica Española* and for her edition and English translation of Bartolomé de las Casas' *History of the Indies,* a seventeenth-century defense of native peoples brutalized by the Spanish conquest of the Americas. She was one of the original founders of the Boston chapter of the National Organization of Women (N.O.W.) and was for many years an active campaigner around women's issues and animal liberation. She died in 1986 before the final work on *Rape of the Wild* was completed.

Joyce Contrucci was born in Pittsburgh, Pennsylvania, in 1946; she received an M.A. in Experimental Psychology in 1970 and a Ph.D. in 1975, both from Ohio State University. She is Assistant Professor of Psychology at Emmanuel College, Boston, Massachusetts, and lectures on the Psychology of Women at Northeastern University. She lived with Andrée Collard from 1980 to 1986, collaborated with her on *Rape of the Wild,* and completed the work after Andrée's death.

ANDRÉE COLLARD

with Joyce Contrucci

Rape of the Wild

**Man's Violence against
Animals and the Earth**

INDIANA UNIVERSITY PRESS
Bloomington and Indianapolis

First published in the United States by Indiana University Press, 1989

Manufactured in the United States of America

Library of Congress Cataloging-in-Publication Data

Collard, Andrée, 1926-1986.
    Rape of the wild.

    Includes index.
        1. Human ecology. 2. Feminist criticism.
    3. Animals, Treatment of. 4. Philosophy of nature.
    I. Construcci, Joyce.   II. Title.
    GF50.C63 1988   179' .1   88-32042
    ISBN 0-253-31514-X
    ISBN 0-253-20519-0 (pbk.)

            1 2 3 4 5 93 92 91 90 89

I dedicate this book to my mother, who showed
me the ways of animals and the earth, and how
to love them; and to the memory of my father,
who showed me that ideals could be real

to Joyce, whose keen, searching mind, whose generous,
life-giving spirit breathes throughout these pages

to the en-souled creatures of the earth, who
have suffered and died at the hands of man

and to the wonder of this Earth, the wilderness.

(A.C.)

And to the Tilia tree.
(J.C.)

Contents

Foreword

Andrée Collard's *Rape of the Wild* is a remarkable book. Its power has its source in the unique integrity of its author, who Spun this work out of the Passion of her own be-ing and love for Life. *Rape of the Wild* conveys her Rage against the destroyers of women and nature. This Rage is as lucid as it is profound. It is rooted in her exquisite sensitivity to the lives of all creatures. During the course of our long friendship (I first met Andrée at a N.O.W. meeting in 1969), I witnessed countless instances of this sensitivity – toward raccoons, cats, dogs, ants, geese, roses, cucumbers, tall pines, birds, bugs, and their multitudinous companions on this beautiful Earth. Indeed, the spider who by 'coincidence' just arrived yesterday at my desk and is presently swinging from the lamp over my typewriter as I write this is an appropriate reminder of this history.

I find it hard to Name the unusual quality of Andrée's intelligent and complex love and respect for nature without appearing to exaggerate the case. In fact, any seeming exaggeration is likely to be mere understatement. How can I say it clearly enough? She *really cared* what happened to any bird or beetle that crossed her path. This was not sentimentality. If anything, it was tough-mindedness, forcing her to face the problems posed to one who saw what she saw, felt what she felt, and struggled to live with integrity in this patriarchal society.

I think that *Rape of the Wild* is one of the really significant books that have come out of the women's movement. In this book, Andrée Collard Names with uncompromising Courage the evil wrought by the patriarchal rapers of Earth. *Rape of the Wild* is a major work of ecofeminism, demonstrating and explaining the unity of women and nature and the oneness of women's struggle to save our Selves and to save the planet. It makes absolutely clear the connections between ecology and Radical Feminism. Its author was able to do this because she Lived both of these causes to the utmost of her not inconsiderable capacity.

I like to think of *Rape of the Wild* as a kind of holophrase. Andrée herself was very fond of this word and – drawing from Jane Ellen Harrison – she explains that a holophrase 'verbalises the way a healthy mind perceives experience and expresses it without separating emotion and reason, feeling and thought, self and non-self'. In this book she struggles to Name and transcend the obstacles embedded in the non-holophrastic, hierarchical syntax and vocabulary of the language she was obliged to speak and write.

Andrée Collard's holophrastic way of thinking* made her an astute critic of English and other European languages. In fact, linguistic criticism plays an important part in her ecofeminist analysis because 'the hierarchical structure of Western societies – therefore of their languages – is antagonistic to the expression of . . . wholesomeness'. *Rape of the Wild* demonstrates this antagonism. The reader of this book will find many striking examples of the degradation of nature, and especially of the un-souling of animals – in these languages. Such degradation is inherent in patriarchal speech, for: 'Man named himself by an act of separation from and power over nature, animals and women'. Exorcising the distortions propagated by such language is required, for they corrupt our very souls. 'The importance of language can hardly be overrated since, as one acquires a language, one acquires the mental dispositions implicit in it.'

This holophrastic work is utterly Other than mere 'issues'-oriented feminism and ecology which fail to Name the connections between women and nature as well as connections among the atrocities perpetrated under patriarchy against all life. Andrée Collard makes it clear that 'father-rule tears morality out of the fabric of social conscience', that it destroys the moral relationship with nature by transferring loyalties from *nature* to *nation*. Since nations need defence, protection, and war, they reduce people to rallying around arbitrarily

---

* Holophrastic or polysynthetic languages, such as Eskimo, are such that 'many of the elements of a sentence or phrase are combined into one utterance and do not exist separately' (*American Heritage Dictionary*, under *polysynthetic*). I use *holophrastic* in a wide sense here to Name the holistic way of perceiving and speaking that characterised Andrée and her work.

chosen symbols, such as flags and heroes. Andrée goes to the root of the problem(s) – patriarchal culture, which defines adulthood in terms of one's ability to separate from mother/nature and which therefore is bound to be destructive. A key theme running through *Rape of the Wild* is that we have seen the world too long through the eyes of men. Thus social scientists glorify hunting as a major evolutionary step, thereby justifying a culture of brutality toward and rape of all that is viewed as 'fair game'. Andrée's envisioning of an ancient matriarchal gathering culture which could have generated a far greater evolutionary leap is inspiring. It exercises the feminist imagination. I agree with her view that such alternative theorising about the remote past is vital for women regaining a sense of our Selves and our own values. Some of us can recall the incredible impact that Elizabeth Gould Davis's *The First Sex* had upon feminists in the early 1970s. I can still see the face of one student as she exclaimed: 'What if women really *were* the first sex!' I could veritably see layers of mindbindings fall away from that woman's consciousness.

The chapter on animal experimentation is extremely difficult to read – and it is essential to read it. The horrors exposed are deeply shocking, and any woman still in touch with her ability to think and feel deeply can never see 'our' society in the same comfortable old ways after reading this material. Andrée demonstrates the condition of animal experimenters as 'seeing through the eyes of the dead'. In this chapter she shouts through the walls of psychic numbing, exposing what she Names 'the banality of cruelty' in this society, showing that this is comparable to what the scientists call 'low-level' radiation and 'low-level' carcinogens.

Andrée Collard does not fail to make completely clear the relevance of animal experimentation to women. Her analogy between the torture of Pavlov's dogs and the everyday torture of women is stunning, and her comparison of trafficking in animals by animal breeders to the slave and prostitute trades is thought-provoking. I find it hard to believe that any woman can be unshaken by the implications of her analysis of the chain of manufactured false needs in which animals are the targets of research and women are the targets of marketing of products (such as dietetic beverages and make-up) whose lethal consequences 'require' further animal research.

This book contains many illuminating examples of the omnipresent patriarchal device of reversal. Noting that 'health' is commonly given as a rationalisation for animal experimentation, the author points out: 'If health were a genuine concern, scientists would turn their minds to restoring healthy conditions for all life.' Moreover: 'Inducing disease in animals is an unhealthy act both for the agent (the experimenter) and the victim. By definition, un-health cannot bring about health.' One of the most colossal reversals is the animal researchers' use of 'happiness' as a rationalisation for their hideous activities: 'Those who chart and stimulate the brain, splice and recombine genes, manipulate environments so as to modify behaviour, hybridise species and attempt to couple man with machine always point to "happiness" as their ultimate goal.'

Their mind-twisting ill-logic serves both to hide and to expose the mentality of the sadists who pose as promoters of 'health' and 'happiness'. It is essential that women see through their legitimations, for 'what has been done to animals has always preceded what has been done to us'. Especially now, in the face of the mounting horror of reproductive technologies as these encroach upon women's lives, refusal to see amounts to passive acceptance of gynocide.

The call of this book is really the Call of the Wild. It is not only a rational plea; it is a roar. It seems impossible to me that any reader could fail to hear this roaring. Andrée Collard calls to feminists and ecologists alike, impatiently pointing out that if we are to achieve any *real* gains in eliminating our oppression, it will be through a recollection of our lost identity. To reiterate her own words:

> I think it is time to put ecology back into feminism . . . Otherwise the supremacist mentality that rules the affairs of our planet will continue to run its destructive course and annihilate us all in the name of health, happiness, and progress.

It is because of this split between ecology and feminism that 'reading ecologists is maddeningly depressing'. Indeed this must be the case as long as they are unable to Name the patriarchal roots of the problem. Despite the efforts of Commoner *et al.* to discuss and mend 'the broken connection', ecology alone cannot Name and mend the broken bonds between women and nature.

It is up to women to do such Naming and mending – especially those who are feminists in the most radical sense. *Rape of the Wild* is a beacon for the consciousness of such women. It summons all readers to Weave and Re-weave the broken connections, defy the foolish phallocrats, and move on. Otherwise the hunters, experimenters, torturers, maimers, killers of women, animals, and nature will go on and on, lurching ahead on their evil and insane tracks, tracking us down, camouflaging their cruelty with reversals and soul-killing banality.

Regaining our powers to Name and to mend requires facing the fact that atrocities are actually happening. Hundreds of millions of animals are being bred to undergo intense pain in animal experimentation. Nuclearism and chemical contamination are really here. The wilderness is being destroyed. When I was returning home by plane after giving a lecture in Pennsylvania recently, I was treated to a real life double feature: the plane circled near Three Mile Island, allowing a perfect 'bird's eye' view of this horror. As I recoiled from this, the man seated next to me initiated a monologue in my direction, informing me that he cuts hundreds of acres of timber in Maine for a living. When he recovered from my tastefully snarled rebuke, he explained that he was a fundamentalist and that the bible says the world will end in a few years anyway. Meanwhile he is a good christian and puts bread on the table for his family. What's wrong with that? I will not print the sentence with which I concluded his monologue. Suffice it to say that he slumped quietly in his seat and my Creative Rage and humour were refuelled. If only I could learn to do all of my travelling by broom!

Meanwhile, space is 'the latest wilderness slated for colonisation'. Andrée Collard's sardonic humour and sense of absolute outrage are nowhere more obvious than in the last section of this book: 'Space colonies: the great escape'. After discussing the function of science fiction films in preparing the public for attempts at space colonisation she reminds us of the actual horrors involved in such plans. The manufacturing of 'monsters' suited for space travel will mean more and more animal suffering. It also implies more tinkering with women's bodies by the new reproductive technologists. It means the robotisation of life.

As I write this Foreword, I have next to my typewriter a copy of the *Boston Globe* (11 August, 1987) which flashes the front-page headline: 'US, Soviets renew joint space study'. Of course, they intend to lurch on and on. Alice Walker puts the case very nicely,

Naming the lust of white men 'to dominate, exploit, and despoil not just our planet but the rest of the universe, which is their clear and oft-stated intention'. After considering the possibility of 'accepting our demise as a planet as a simple and just preventive medicine administered to the universe' she decides that since life is better than death, and since earth is her home (despite the efforts of white people to negate this fact), she intends to protect her home.[1]

Rape of the Wild is a Call to women to protect our home.

Andrée Collard's part in the women's movement is to awaken women's consciousness/conscience concerning nature. Her feminism/ecology was not just a 'cause' to her. It was her life. In addition to being the author of *Rape of the Wild*, she was a farmer and beekeeper, as well as professor of romance languages and comparative literature at Brandeis University. She was a woman of many gifts. She was cut down before seeing her work come to fruition.

In a recent conversation with Joyce Contrucci, we talked about our sense that it is a crime that Andrée's book had to be published posthumously. My grief and rage are mingled with hope that her message will be heard. It is Time. I hope also that readers will sense throughout this difficult work the enormous *joie de vivre* of its author, whose Passion for living is the source of the lucidity and outrage expressed in these pages.

If women rouse ourSelves from the effects of the planned, systematic moronisation and psychic numbing inflicted by 'our' culture, we can learn to participate in the powers of the Goddess Nemesis, bringing about Elemental disruption of the patriarchal balance of terror. We can Passionately Spin New and Archaic threads of Gynergy. I believe that Andrée Collard is Present, together with Other Foresisters and Spirits of the universe, as women summon the Courage to do our own work on this planet, Realising our Lust for Happiness, continuing the Journey, always.

Mary Daly
Newton Center, Massachusetts
15 August 1987

Notes

1. Alice Walker, 'Only justice can stop a curse', *In Search of Our Mothers' Gardens* (San Diego, Ca: Harcourt, Brace, Jovanovich, 1983; London: The Women's Press, 1984), pp. 341–2.

Acknowledgments

This book grew out of a speech I gave on 8 April 1979 in Morse Auditorium, Boston University, at *The Event* organised in support of Mary Daly when she was being harassed by Boston College subsequent to the publication of her book *Gyn/Ecology* in 1978. It was Mary who originally suggested and encouraged me to formalise my work on nature, animals and women into a book.

Since then many women have helped and supported me through the process of writing *Rape of the Wild*. In the early stages of 'jumping in' in 1979, Kristine Kazie and Maria Marques contributed a lot of perspicacious suggestions and generous support. Isabel van den Heuvel provided a steady flow of useful information and, as 'the book' took firmer, more distinct shape through 1980, Joan Hartel, Eileen Barrett, Denise Connors and Diana Davies continued to provide resource material.

Many women gave tangible support without which my writing would have been impossible. Judy Trudgen helped maintain the physical order and comfort so needed during critical stages of writing. She always appeared at the darkest moments, most often unasked and, without fanfare, created livable working space out of chaos and confusion. This was especially true during my preparation for and eventual move to Norwell in 1980. She, along with Barbara Zanotti, Jackie de Vincent, Leslie Dubinsky and Fran Challand, added their gynergy, humour and encouragement to that physical transition which could have halted work on the book entirely. In a similar vein, I want to give special acknowledgment to the late poet Beatrice Hawley, who, during the early phase of writing, appeared at my door many times with nourishing meals and refreshing, genuine conversation.

Among the women who believed in my work and the importance of naming the parallels between the exploitation and degradation of animals and women were Janice Raymond and Renate Duelli-Klein who, in addition, facilitated access to The Women's Press. Linda Barifauldi gave thoughtful, sensitive reading and insightful commentary to early drafts of the first three chapters. Anne Dellenbaugh provided skilful editorial assistance with Chapter 1 in preparation for its publication in *Trivia* (Spring 1983).

Andrée Collard

These are the acknowledgments which Andrée Collard left in late 1985 before *Rape of the Wild* was in final publication form. Since her death in 1986 I have received noteworthy assistance in completing this book which I want to acknowledge.

At the time when our world split apart at Andrée's death, Fran Chelland rose, with incredible strength and courage, through her shock and grief, to do *inestimable* editorial work on Chapters 2, 3, 4 and 5. I want to acknowledge Fran's work not only for the fine, intellectual contribution it made to *Rape of the Wild*, but also as an act of pure, unselfish devotion to the life and memory of Andrée Collard. Mary Daly, Andrée's loyal friend, was a constant presence during all this work and gave generously of her time and gynergy. I am also deeply grateful to Mary for the many times when, putting aside her own grief and rage, she heard my grief into words and steadied my soul so that I could work.

My family – Joe, Peg, Judith, Joelene, Joel and Elizabeth, my mother – kept loud and clear faith in my abilities and vision and insisted on my right to actualise them both. Each stood around me as a veritable pillar of strength. Crystal Chemris, Denise Donnelly, Kristine Kazie and Maja Goth, by their deep understanding and wholehearted support of me, helped to free my power for the task at hand.

Charlotte Raymond, literary agent, guided me through some tough straits in the publication world and helped me avoid pitfalls I was not even aware existed. Jen Green was a sensitive and patient managing editor in shepherding the book toward publication. Janet Tyrrell, copy editor, went through the manuscript with a fine-toothed comb which I, at times, prayed would break a few teeth. Fortunately, it did not and the book is better for her ruthless attention to detail. On a moment's notice, Suanne Scalise graciously made proofreading a priority in her life and less of a strain in mine.

I want to acknowledge the daily companionship of the plants and animals, both inside and outside the house, who gave me comfort and concrete reasons to continue.

Finally and ultimately, I acknowledge the wild and glorious spirit of Andrée Collard, without whose love and light this book would not be.

Joyce Contrucci
Norwell, Massachusetts
27 February 1988

Rape of the Wild

Introduction

Susan B. Anthony once asked why women did not burn with outrage and protest at the discrimination of rights and privilege they faced because of their sex. In the past fifteen years, feminists have developed methodologies with which to analyse sexism, fuel protest, and foster liberation. In reclaiming the power to name ourselves and our experiences, women have exposed patriarchy as a disease. The treatment of nature and animals is the vilest manifestation of that disease. Nature and animals communicate their plight in ways this culture refuses to understand. This book is a burning protest against the violation of nature and animals which in patriarchy is inextricably connected with the oppression of women. Feminists must articulate this oppression as part of our holistic, biophilic vision.* For it is a fact that no woman will be free until all animals are free and nature is released from man's ruthless exploitation.

In patriarchy, nature, animals and women are objectified, hunted, invaded, colonised, owned, consumed and forced to yield and to produce (or not). This violation of the integrity of wild, spontaneous Being is rape. It is motivated by a fear and rejection of Life and it allows the oppressor the illusion of control, of power, of being alive. As with women as a class, nature and animals have been kept in a state of inferiority and powerlessness in order to enable men as a class to believe and act upon their 'natural' superiority/dominance.

I have used animals as a window to the death-oriented values of

* 'Biophilic', as originally used by Mary Daly, literally means 'life-loving'. See Mary Daly, *Gyn/Ecology: The Metaethics of Radical Feminism* (Boston: Beacon Press, 1978; London: The Women's Press, 1979), p. 10. For an expanded definition, see Mary Daly, *Websters' First New Intergalactic Wickedary of the English Language* (Boston: Beacon Press, 1987; London: The Women's Press, 1988), p.67.

patriarchal society partly from a deep concern for their wellbeing and partly because man's treatment of them exposes those values in their crudest, most undisguised form. I have taken the position that it is morally wrong to kill for pleasure, to inflict pain for the thrill of discoveries nobody needs, to colonise other creatures' minds and bodies, to make a fetish of those very animals the culture as a whole is bent on eliminating, and to conserve wild animals in parks, zoos and game reserves, thereby destroying their integrity of being. Likewise, apathy, thoughtlessness, and the denial of responsibility and choice are moral transgressions; they allow for the overall pollution and destruction of the earth, the oppression of people, the atrocities committed on animals in laboratories in the name of scientific progress, and the objectification of wildlife in general through conservation programmes and domestication.

Because rape of the wild and the free spirit of nature is complex and painful, a number of emotions which I have made little attempt to disguise have gone into this book. I am first of all always on the side of nature. Her innocence (in the etymological sense of 'not noxious') may derive from the fact that she acts not from choice but from inherent need. Whatever nature does that seems cruel and evil to anthropomorphising eyes is done without intent to harm. Nature has worked out a self-regulated flow of birth and decay, striking a balance between death and rejuvenation which human beings in their propagating folly ought to have taken as a model. Where the human hand has not greedily tinkered, nature is spontaneous, awesome, refreshingly unselfconscious, magnificently diverse. For thousands of years, nature has been the measure of our humanity, providing much of our self-identity.

I do not believe in trying to reverse time and 'go primitive', but it is important to broaden our understanding of the past and learn from other cultures and other times the way of universal kinship. By universal kinship I mean a recognition on the part of all individuals of our common bond with all that exists. This recognition would lead to an understanding/feeling that the most 'insignificant' part is indispensable to the harmony and wellbeing of the whole. In other words, it would put human beings back into the concept and reality of nature as similar, and leave behind the concept of nature as different and inferior. It would impart dignity to our dealings with all creatures by dissolving the patriarchal separatist mentality that fractures life into inimical factions. It would abolish all divisive 'isms' – sexism, racism, classism, ageism, militarism, etc. In short, acting upon the concept of universal kinship would start the cultural revolution that would be the undoing of patriarchy.

1. Rape of the wild

Beauty and grace are performed whether or not we
will or sense them. The least we can do is try to be
there.

Annie Dillard, *Pilgrim at Tinker Creek*

Why doesn't the white man accept things as they are
and leave the world alone?

Aunt Queen James, Native American

What is nature?

The answer to that question is a matter of cultural and personal training, occupational bias, and experience. In the West today, most people are apt to point to 'everything out there', regardless of what is in
front of their eyes – a city park, a college campus, a garden. Nature is
everything from mountain trail to 'biomass', beaches, birds and bees,
sunshine and petunias.

Nature is still occasionally referred to as 'Mother Nature',
although the phrase no longer reflects its original meaning. It retains a
vague connotation of uncontrollably punishing weather in the
language of weather forecasters. It stirs up fantasies of conquest in
the language of hunters who claim to 'love' nature even as they kill
her animals. It obsesses all manner of scientists who 'love' her to
death in an attempt to 'penetrate' and 'understand' all her secrets.
Mother Nature is one thing to lovers, another to scientists, farmers,
bricklayers, office workers, land developers, and so on.

It is clear that the word 'nature' does not so much define *what* we
see but *how* we see. The hunter loves not nature but how he feels *in* it

as he stalks his prey. The animal experimenter loves not animals but the feeling of power and importance he derives from controlling them. Thus nature is a state of mind and a cultural convention. The external world exists in and of itself but the words by which it is known state the quality of our relationship with it. In Western cultures, this relationship is utilitarian and exploitative.

Moreover, we tend to think of nature as the antithesis of culture, on the grounds that nature makes itself while culture is man-made. The wilderness, by definition unknown, untamed, untouched by human contact, is the antithesis of culture. However, when it becomes part of human experience, the wilderness becomes a part of nature, which is equivalent to saying that it becomes an aspect of culture. The explorers of unknown territory take with them a set of values and attitudes that inform the definition of the wild. This is true of all migrations and individual expeditions, as well as of such enterprises as the conquest of the New World, the American Frontier, and outer space. Where direct experience of the wilderness is lacking, human imagination draws upon cultural images and/or fantasy to describe it, as is the case with those poets, philosophers and fiction writers who never venture beyond their civilised surroundings yet soar well above them in their works.

It is precisely the projection of cultural values upon the external world that determines the treatment meted out to it. In the beginning and in some societies today, human relationship to nature was and is intensely sacred. In all countries influenced by the West, it is intensely destructive. We inherited the word 'nature' from those beginnings but, as the word rolled on the tongues of countless generations down to us, it has become a catch-all, a degutted sound, much like its 'professional' synonyms: environment, ecosystem, biosphere, etc.

Naming

> In the beginning was the Word.
>
> (John 1:1)

To name is to place oneself in relation to what is being named, to give it value, and to shape it. A name is nothing less than an existential statement about the people who invent it. It is important to keep in mind the connection between social organisations and language.

Otherwise, we risk falling into the trap set by language theoreticians who on the whole tend to tear words and syntax out of the socio-emotional context in which they developed. Thus students of linguistic phenomena are never asked to confront the past in a way that would demand a stretching of the imagination to include questions about the *quality* of life reflected in language, and, in the case that concerns me here, about the quality of life reflected in the word 'nature'.

It is likely that, in its origin, 'nature' was not a word in our sense but a statement expressing an experience of the external world. Such statements are called holophrases.[1] Just as human experience of the external world is changeable and varied, so there would be a number of different holophrases conveying a sense of nature. Native American languages give us a good idea of how this verbalisation functions. Speaking about the importance of a mountain in the endangered California Siskiyou country, an old Indian woman of the region said:

> You come upon a place you've never seen before, and it has awesome beauty, everything above you, below you, around you is so pure – that is the beauty we call *merwerksergerh*, and the pure person is also *merwerksergerh*.[2]

'Merwerksergerh' is a holophrase which expresses one aspect of the complex living relationship between the Native American and 'nature'. The difference between holophrases and the syntax of European languages is enormously important. Rape of the wild, that is, the insatiable appetite to control nature by systematically destroying it, is inconceivable in societies whose speech is experiential and non-analytical.

Holophrases are possible only in societies where the sense of 'we' is greater than the sum of individual 'I's'. This 'we-ness' includes all of nature, which is responded to rather than acted upon. 'Merwerksergerh' is a statement of simultaneous thinking and feeling. What is being seen ('a place') is not evaluated as a separate object but is one with the person who experiences it. There is no 'I' distinct from the pure, awesome beauty of the place. English syntax, as well as that of all European languages, requires an agent acting upon an object and giving it value. It requires the object to be situated with respect to the agent. Thus the object is always circumstantial, literally meaning that it 'stands around' the agent, and is separated from it by a number of parts of speech: the place is *above*, *below*, *around* 'you' and 'you' are the agent/spectator by virtue of your language which breaks down (analyses) and weighs everything according to proportions (ratio) relative to the individual 'I'.

In her discussion of holophrases, classicist Jane Harrison emphasised the intimate correspondence between language and social structure. She pointed out that a holophrase verbalises a holopsychosis (*holo*, whole; *psychosis*, a giving of life), that is, it verbalises the way a healthy mind perceives experience and expresses it without separating emotion and reason, feeling and thought, self and non-self.[3] The hierarchical structure of Western societies – therefore of their languages – is antagonistic to the expression of this wholesomeness. Hierarchy divides and fragments. It functions on the strength of linear, rational discourse. Thus, in Western languages, oneness with the non-self and other integrated experiences are difficult to verbalise.[4]

Nature as Mother and Goddess

Nature is a modern word that belongs to the rational discourse of patriarchy. We have it from the Latin (*natus*: born) which took the concept from the Greeks (*physis*: nature – from *phyein*: to bring forth). That which is born is born of someone – the Primal Ancestress, the Old One or mother figure of the Palaeolithic Age (25,000–15,000 BC) which by the Neolithic Age (8000–3000 BC) became identified as Mother Earth, the creative power of the universe. Being born of Mother Earth, everything that existed was perceived as partaking of her spirit and there developed a relationship of kinship between human beings and all of creation – vegetation, animals, the elements, and other planets. This holistic approach to life is thought to have originated in Mesopotamia, spreading throughout the Near and Middle East, Europe, Africa, and Asia. The creation stories of Native Americans throughout the continent make it clear that this relationship was universal. Earth worship persisted officially up to AD 500 in Europe[5] and persists today among those Native American tribes who choose to remain in their own traditions.

European-based societies receive their notion of Mother Earth from pre-Hellenic Greece influenced by Crete, Ancient Anatolia and the Near East, as well as from the powerful Celtic tradition which extends in a broad sweep from northern Ireland to Spain. The contribution of the Etruscans has not been sufficiently examined. However, their highly sophisticated drawings suggest the primacy of the female in ways reminiscent of Cretan art.

Earth/Goddess worship is always a sign of matriarchal organisation. I want to stress this point, known to and much discussed among feminists, because as women we are nothing without the memory of our past. As an academic, I am aware that 'Women's Studies' offer information about the history of women in the patriarchy. This is not enough. The history of women's oppression must continually be juxtaposed with what came before. Only then can we have a vision of what we were and therefore what we can be. The lack of this knowledge encourages women to want incorporation into man's world on an 'equality' basis, meaning that woman absorbs his ideologies, myths, history, etc. and loses all grounding in her own traditions. As Anne Cameron said, 'There is a better way of doing things. Some of us remember that way.'[6] This better way includes kinship, egalitarianism,[7] and nurturance-based values which women experienced and projected not only on their goddesses but on to every creature among them. By contrast, when men invented their gods, they projected on to them isolated individualism, hierarchical relationships and power-based values which are reflected in patriarchal social arrangements.

Earth worship corresponds to what textbooks summarily call animism, namely, the belief that everything that lives is endowed with soul/spirit. Animism is always labelled primitive, and 'primitive' carries a host of negative connotations only because the reference point used is our so-called advanced stage of civilisation.

Animism extended to plants and animals because of the spiritual power (mana) they were perceived to have as children of the Earth Mother. As the agricultural 'revolution' (dated at about 7000 BC) brought more experiences of the animal and plant worlds, the accompanying expansion of consciousness was reflected in an expanded vocabulary as well as in an expanded concept of the Goddess. While continuing to be represented in her more ancient forms, the bird and the snake, she was then believed to dwell in olives and barley, the cow and the pig.

Creatures as diverse to us as the pig, the dolphin and the human child were perceived as uterine animals: animals born of the same mother, nourished at the same source, subject to the same laws. They came to be called animals because they were en-souled. The word 'animal' is based on the Latin *anima* (soul). Likewise the Greek *Zōion* (animal) is based on *zōē*, life – everyone's life. The soul, in any language, is the life principle itself which gives everything the atmosphere in which to grow. At death, humans and animals return to 'live' underground in the earth's bosom that gave them birth.

Festivals of vegetation – edible roots, nuts, wild fruit-bearing trees – existed throughout the Middle East well before and into the agricultural revolution. They continued into the Bronze Age (roughly the second millennium BC) in societies that succeeded in maintaining the religion of the Goddess. Legume ('that which is gathered') is a word related to *logos* which means 'the essence of being' in its archaic sense. Fruit ('that which is enjoyable') is connected to the concepts of enjoyment and harvest. Vegetables vegetate, that is, they grow, rouse, excite. In its etymological sense, vegetable refers to the growth process, to the ripening of corn and grain, to the coming of age. The maiden becomes mother. Such is the meaning of Demeter ('De' is a linguistic variant of 'Ge', which means 'earth'; 'meter' means 'mother'), whose Latin name, Ceres, gives the word cereal.

Behind the naming of legumes, fruit, vegetable, and grain, we find the same element of mutuality that inspired the naming of animals. The reciprocity between the people and the thing named means that vegetables were perceived as rising in excitement just as they were exciting; fruit was believed to enjoy growing just as it was enjoyable; 'legume' gathered life and gave life as it was gathered; and animals were animated (en-souled) and animating as all shared a common soul with humans through the Earth Mother. This participatory, reverential attitude toward nature was highly moral because it was customary ('moral' comes from Latin *mos*: custom) but most of all it was moral in our sense because humans recognised the value of every life form and respected it.

The Triple Goddess

Ancient cultures gave magical power to certain numbers which unravelled, protected, and contained the essence of the phenomena most important to them. Among Native Americans, that number seems to be four. In the Mediterranean, it is three.

There the Earth Goddess was worshipped in the three aspects inherent in the life-cycle of the women who created her, thus giving rise to the trinitarian concept that was to become the central article of Christian dogma.[8] She validated and dignified woman as maiden (nymph), mother, and crone. She was felt as a real and tangible presence among women. She was 'everything that is' because she brought forth everything into being.

Thus, she was as inseparable from the 'three' phases of the moon (the fourth is invisible) as she was from her plant and animal manifestations. She was Hecate, Selene, Artemis the far-shooting moon. She was Helen, Phoebe, Eurynome the wide-wandering. And she was at the same time Earth, Wind, Water, etc., under a constellation of names that varied according to the languages spoken in the areas where she was worshipped.

As for Pandora, so maligned in the patriarchal version of her myth, she too is the Primitive Matriarch, all-giving, all-knowing, and loved by all. Hidden in her bosom are numerous earth spirits that correspond to human emotion – joy, love, sorrow, loneliness. Her sacred shrine is the hearth, the egg-shaped or beehive-like womb in which the sacred snake dwells as guardian spirit.

In this context, it is interesting to remember how the worshippers of the Goddess named themselves. We think of the mythological giants and titans as aggressive, larger-than-life figures because they appear as such in the Homeric tradition. But, as Jane Harrison has shown, 'giant' means 'earthling', and so does 'titan', that is, creatures born of Ge (Gaia) and Titaia, ancient names of Mother Earth.

Remembering the past

What could today's women learn from these ancient namings, festivals and personifications of the Goddess? We could reasonably conclude that a woman's seal of approval came from herself and other women, not from standards of youth and beauty determined by men to please themselves. In those early societies, make-up and fashions aimed at keeping a woman looking young 'past her prime' would have been inconceivable. Signs of age would have had none of the traumas associated with growing old in patriarchal cultures. Rather, a woman would have acquired self-esteem from her importance in the community, as well as from her functions, which would have changed – but not diminished – as she aged.

Next, we could reasonably conclude that a woman's self-respect was intimately connected to how she felt about her body and her body's functions. The Greek word for moon is *mēn*, which also means month. It is the root word for a woman's menses, menstruation, menopause. Women exquisitely attuned to the moon's influence on the orderliness of seasons in the ring of time as well as on the regulation of tides, crops, and the menstrual cycle would feel no shame about their bodies. Neither would they ridicule the bodies of other women, looking for imperfections that do not exist, yet finding them as they look, not with their own eyes, but with the critical eye of the male.

Finally, we can infer that a woman's strength came from doing. Where there was no strict division of labour along gender lines, woman's skills developed beyond her famed endurance and purveyance of care and wellbeing. She learned the ways of plants. She learned the ways of other creatures of the land, air and sea. She learned them in a spirit of recognition and respect. And with a similar spirit, she partook of them. It is not difficult to imagine the importance of sharing food in societies in which everything is related through a common mother, the Great Goddess, source of the universe. An economy of waste would have no place in a system that makes sacred what it consumes.

The archetypal mother

By whatever name she is called, the Mother Goddess is the archetypal female symbol. What impresses me about her is the ancientness and the range of her religion, as well as the fact that the people of the Palaeolithic Age throughout Europe and Asia possessed the imagination, skills and leisure to fashion her likeness in small clay figures dated around 25,000 BC. I take the discovery of nothing but female figures from that period as evidence of gynocentric societies or matriarchy. By matriarchy I mean not that women were 'the dominant sex' – the notion of dominance is patriarchal – but that female experience determined culture.

Most of what we know about the archetypal mother comes from

Jungian scholars and mythographers who distort her to accommodate their views of 'the eternal feminine'. The same attitude prevails among the anthropologists who have interpreted those small clay figures as cult objects related to fertility and puberty rites, naming them 'Venus figurines'. Whether as the eternal feminine or Venus, eroticism and motherhood are said to be the basic attributes of woman to the exclusion of everything else.

The 'Venus' figure is round enough. Her breasts are like two full moons, her belly seems to contain the world. She is abundance per-sonified, her body brimming with life and the sustenance of life. She conveys the notion of fullness, a far cry from the image of the lean and hairy prehistoric *man* engaged in 'the struggle for survival'. The latter is a fantasy presented as truth in textbooks, together with the impoverished theory that life is the mere development of survival and reproductive 'strategies'.

Life is an experience, not an exercise in warfare. However central fertility (puberty) rites were in those ancient societies, it is important to remember that life in its fullness, no matter how 'primitive', also contains experiences unrelated to offspring and the scrounging for food. The elements of play, unpredictability, feelings of intercon-nectedness with other life forms, ritualised births, deaths, and ancestor worship, are just as vital to life as 'fertility' rites.[9] Thus, 'Venus figures' are likely to symbolise the whole experience of the people who fashioned them. This, to me, is the meaning of the arche-typal mother.

In her image

Merlin Stone extensively discussed the primitive Goddess in the Near and Middle East in *When God Was a Woman*, reproducing pictures of the sculptured and engraved Goddess from 25,000 to 300 BC. These images show the development of the Goddess religion past the advent of agriculture into the patriarchy. But the monumental works on the importance of the Goddess are classicist Jane Harrison's *Pro-legomena to the Study of Greek Religion* (1903), *Themis: A Study of the Social Origins of Greek Religion* (1912), and *Epilegomena to the Study of Greek Religion* (1921), which focus mainly on pre-Hellenic Greece. From a feminist theoretical standpoint, these works are rather timid.[10] Nevertheless, they contain a wealth of information and engravings that point to an astonishingly evolved culture centred around the primacy of the Earth Mother and woman.

I have already mentioned the sacredness of vegetation and animals in earth worship. This, too, is reflected in ancient art, nowhere more profusely than in Crete, where the serpent predominates as the sacred animal par excellence.[11] An early figure portrays the Goddess 'seated upon feline throne' (5750 BC; Stone, *When God Was a Woman*, figure 4). Discovered in Anatolia, she is similar in her roundness to the celebrated 'Venus figurine' of 20,000 centuries earlier. Her hands rest upon the 'felines' – so-called probably because the precise species is not clearly identifiable. She is clearly the all-giving source of life and is quite awesome in her dignity. There is an old (early third millennium) carving of a Sumerian goddess holding what seems to be a palm – or a stylised fruit-bearing tree – in each hand, while an indistinct animal stands close to her skirt on both sides (Stone, figure 7).

One of my favourite pictures is that of a late (second millennium BC) gold signet-ring from Mycenae (Harrison, *Themis*, figure 36). In Harrison's words,

> Here we have the Earth-goddess or her priestess under her great fruit-bearing tree; she holds poppies in her hand; worshippers approach her bearing flowers and leaf-sprays; behind her a woman gathers fruit, while above her is all the glory of Ouranos, Sun and Moon and Milky Way, and down from the sky come the powers of the sky, the thunder in its double manifestation of shield-demon and battle-axe.[12]

This ritual scene is striking to modern eyes accustomed to the disproportionate enlargement and dominance of god/hero figures. Here, the Goddess is indistinguishable in appearance from the women who surround her. She is life-size, neither standing apart from, nor towering over, the women celebrants. She looks as real as the women who offer fruit and flowers to her. She is neither authoritatively stern nor wrathful but smiles, even as her attendants smile, in a way art historians have labelled 'the archaic smile', elusive, inscrutable. In group scenes, Goddess and women face each other with relaxed and graceful gestures, exuding unselfconscious contentment and inner harmony.

Reshaping woman

This ancient gynocentric way of life is lost but it is there for all to see in museums and books of philosophical, religious, and archaeological interest. It is also recorded in numerous myths and stories of American origin, both North and South. Yet the male popularisers of current theories about the development of the human race ignore it. Whether as the subject of special educational television programmes or in mass-produced popularisations, the image of man stands out as doer and maker of culture. He dominates 'reconstructed' scenes of the ancient 'hunter–gatherer' and agricultural periods. *Origins*, by Richard Leakey and Roger Lewin, is a good representation of this bias. It is an award-winning book (Man in His Environment Award, 1977), heralded as combining 'authoritative information with imaginative illustrations' and as functioning 'as a kind of *Roots* – not just for Leakey but for us all'. *Origins* was also a best-seller about 'how man became man'.[13]

And indeed, it is just that: a book about men, for men, the nuclear family, and patriarchal hierarchies. A woman reading *Origins* might well wonder about *her* roots or, for that matter, whether we existed at all, ever, as creatures in our own right. In this book, the naked male is portrayed as sole specimen of the species in its successive phases of development. 'Handsome' too, young and white. When the female is present, and that is seldom, she is part of a mixed group or couple, she tends babies, she helps her searching, competent mate. These 'imaginative illustrations' gradually give way to photographs of selected contemporary hunter–gatherers which, predictably, support the general assumption that civilisation rests heavily on the hunt and that the hunt is an exclusively male occupation.[14] The reason given for this original division of labour is that child-bearing placed too many restrictions on women's freedom of movement,* although 'even with a possible lesser degree of development in visuo-spatial skills, women certainly could have become proficient hunters'.[15]

Pregnancies and child-bearing have a much deeper significance than possible physical restrictions, for they are a woman's link to the

---

* This may be true of nuclear family situations in which the male controls female sexuality and one woman is the only source of child-care. The communal social organisation of 'primitive' groups precludes this possibility.

natural world and the hunted animals that are part of that world. In those communities whose survival depended in part or in whole on animal products, women, obviously unhampered by their child-bearing capabilities, were vitally involved in the process we now misname hunting (an inappropriate word when used to refer to the occasional capture of an animal to ensure survival). The following excerpt illustrates woman's participation in whale-capturing among the Nootka people of Vancouver Island, who for centuries have depended upon whale products for survival.

> No woman would kill a whale. Whales give birth to livin' young, they don't lay eggs like fish. They feed their babies with milk from their breasts, like women, and we never killed them. The man who killed the whale never tasted whale meat from the time of his first kill until after he'd retired as a whaler. And neither did his wife, because he had to be purified and linked to the whale by way of the woman's blood and woman's milk. No one linked to them will eat of them. It is a promise.[16]

The physical and spiritual connections between women and animals expressed in this passage are consonant with the reverence for nature and animals reflected in the carvings, paintings and engravings made over 15,000 years ago, most likely by women. The describing of woman's reproductive capacity as debilitating to her *and* as the root of *man's* hunting and killing traditions denies and distorts these early connections. It also places the responsibility for the emergence of violence in human societies upon women. I suggest that the reasons for man's predatory relationship to nature can and must be found elsewhere.

The degradation of nature in language

No one knows for sure when men started to challenge the power of the Goddess and set about a long history of subjugation of women, desecration of temples, and destruction of those animals that had been sacred to her. The recorded appearance of god-worshipping males – variously called Indo-Europeans, Indo-Aryans, and Aryans – in the Middle East some 6,000 years ago suggests older beginnings since they are said to have come from north of the Caucasus. At any rate, their language is significant because, together with the assimilation of many linguistic substrata, it evolved into Sanskrit, which, as one of the oldest written languages, provided most of our root words via Greek and Latin.

What happened to nature during this long struggle is documented in language, myth, and literature. The importance of language can hardly be overrated since, as one acquires a language, one acquires the mental dispositions implicit in it. Sanskrit reflects the power relationships which led to the subordination of earth-worshipping peoples and, consequently, to the subordination of the female power of the universe – the Goddess manifested in nature. In the new language (Sanskrit), under the new order (patriarchy), nature and women are reduced from a position of importance to a position of insignificance. In India, where Sanskrit developed, the politics of language includes racial discrimination as well. As Merlin Stone has noted, the words 'light' and 'dark' first acquired the connotations of good and evil in Sanskrit, reflecting the emergent caste system and the Aryans' contempt for the darker-skinned peoples who inhabited India before their arrival.[17]

The Sanskrit word for nature is *prakritri*, 'the natural condition or state of anything, nature, the original source of the material world'. Sometimes personified as the supreme creative power of the universe, it is female in gender and identified with other female energy principles such as *shakti* (power, energy) and *māyā* (the illusory nature of the material world). Another word, *prākrit*, meaning 'natural, unaltered, common, vulgar, unrefined, illiterate, insignificant, trifling' is related to *prakritri* by the same root word. *Prākrit* is also the language of the common people, the conquered people. In contrast the word 'sanskrit' means 'perfected, well-spoken, refined'; it is the language of the people in power, the invaders/conquerers who devalued *prākrit* by disqualifying it as unrefined, imperfect, illiterate, etc. By association, nature (*prakritri*) is also devalued as imperfect.[18]

In the Book of Genesis (first millennium BC), a document that codifies in writing many strands of older oral traditions, the intent to suppress the Great Mother (Ishtar, Inanna, Ti'âmat, etc.) is very clear. Some practices of her cult are openly condemned as they clash with the monotheistic, male tradition of the Hebrews. Mostly, they are omitted. An earlier version of the Genesis creation myth attributes a spirit of rebellion to the first woman, Lilith. In the later version, which we all know, Lilith is replaced by Eve, made of clay together with Adam in one story (Gen. 1:26), born of Adam's rib and made submissive to him in another (Gen. 2:23).

Genesis presents the view that God created everything and gave it to man to dominate. The degrees of his domination range from benevolent stewardship, to conquest (Gen. 1:28) and outright oppression.

Be the terror and the dread of all the wild beasts and all the birds of heaven, of everything that crawls on the ground and all the fish of the sea. (Gen. 9:2-3)

Moreover, since God creates nature, nature is everything in the universe that existed before the appearance of human beings. By the same token, it is everything that man cannot create. Envy of Mother Earth is expressed by projecting upon God the ability to create life. The solution is to erase the Goddess. Before 'the beginning' to which Genesis refers, 'the earth was a formless void' (Gen. 1: 1-2).

A few thousand years later, the writers of the Gospels gathered what suited Christianity from the Old Testament. They kept nature and women in a position of subordination to man. St John understood the power of the act of naming which is adumbrated in Genesis: 'These he [God] brought to the man to see what he would call them; each one was to bear the name the man would give it' (Gen. 2:20). For John, 'In the beginning was the Word: the Word was with God and the Word was God' (John 1:1). In this context, a thing exists only as and when it exists in God's consciousness. God is given the power of language as he pulls creation out of nothingness and names it. 'In the beginning' clearly refers to the beginning of god worship and cancels everything that came before (goddess worship) by not mentioning it.

Meanwhile, the Greeks had also been busy dismantling the old cults and renaming nature. As in modern usage, for Aristotle *physis* (nature) has none of the associations with the female power of the universe, although it derives from the verb meaning 'to give birth, to bring forth'. For him, *physis* is a secular word, referring to the 'physical' (natural) phenomena the human senses can observe and measure. It is inferior to *technē* – the root word of 'technology' – which designates the skilful imitation of an object. Such artefacts are deemed superior to anything which *physis*, in her irrationality, is able to bring forth. Just as Sanskrit 'corrected' and 'refined' *prākrit*, so *technē* corrects and refines *physis*. Thus the Greeks declared man the master of nature (and woman), and established the superiority of reason and technology.

The consequences of rejecting identification with nature and adopting a stance detached from it are of incalculable magnitude for us. Seventeenth-century Europe, believed to be the turning point in the evolution of Western thought toward scientific 'objectivity' that spelled the death of nature,[19] is in reality the consummate expression of the power relationships and devaluation of nature inherent in Sanskrit. 'Perfect, refine, and improve upon nature' was the dictum under which baroque art flourished. In other fields of endeavour, 'improvement' and 'invention' contributed technological 'advances' which in turn were predicated on man's faith in his god-given right to use nature as he saw fit. Thus, one thing leading to another, the tradition that turned nature into a 'superior', technological product at the hands of man led to the culture of artefacts, the artificial culture we live in today which is destroying the world.

Reductionistic language

Reductionism is detachment taken a step further. It is the result of the inability to respond to life with aesthetic emotion. Carried into language, this approach yields a mathematical science based on the mechanics of transmitting information for manipulative purposes rather than on the very real art of communicating experience which is the base of all authentic knowledge. Not surprisingly, computer 'language' derives from such studies.

When the mind takes to the habit of abstracting things (and words) from their reality, then *anyone*'s reality can be superimposed on them, including one that is at the very opposite end of what the word is supposed to convey. This is the mechanism of Orwell's *Newspeak*, and it is common enough. For example, in his award-winning *Lives of a Cell*, Lewis Thomas reflects on the etymological connection between 'gene', 'nature', and 'physics'.

These days it is reassuring to know that nature and physics, *in their present meanings*, have been interconnected in our minds, *by a sort of hunch*, for all these years. The other words clinging to them *are a puzzlement*, but *nice* to see. If you let your mind relax, all the words will flow into each other in an amiable sort of nonsense.[20] (emphases added)

Those other 'puzzling' words are 'kin', 'kind', and 'gentle'. If anything, the study of etymology invites detective work around the word itself. How were those connections made? To what does the cluster refer? Who were the speakers? Who was the intended audience? In this case, 'gene', 'nature', *'physis'*, 'kin', 'kind', and 'gentle' all refer to Mother Earth. If, like Thomas, we believe that words 'simply turn up in the language as they are needed',[21] then anything goes, even the most flagrant contradictions in terms. It is shocking to invite readers to relax into such armchair vagaries while *physics* is irradiating nature *(physis)* out of existence.

Words do not make themselves up and draw their own associations haphazardly. At the very least, words live in the subconscious of the namer in response to a phenomenon. The namer then makes associations and articulates the new word. In the case of 'physics', all it means is the activity that seeks to know the things of nature. However, in the reductionist sense of information gathered from breaking those things to pieces, physics is an ongoing re-enactment of the rape of nature.

Like Virginia Woolf, I believe that good words have an aura, an evocative power. I like the way Louise B. Young describes the aura of life forms – to which I would add the aura of words – in her book about the destruction of the ozone layer that protects the earth's atmosphere from the sun's radioactivity.

Every life form has an aura characteristic of its personality; a breath, a scent, and a flow of energy emanate from it. This luminous cloud may be fragrant and radiant, or sour and dull, depending upon the inner life of the organism.[22]

And, although she uses 'man' in the 'generic' sense and I use it specifically to denote the men and women who uphold patriarchal values, I agree with her that 'man's aura is becoming darker and more bitter year by year'.

The degradation of nature as Goddess

The literature that was evolving in Mesopotamia during the Indo-

European invasions is brutally clear about the fate of nature, animals, and women, as the Goddess who includes them all is destroyed. The Gilgamesh Epic, the national epic of the Babylonian Semites composed about 2000 BC, provides a good example of this literature. Like all narratives of its kind, the Gilgamesh Epic is the end product of an oral tradition which combines fact and fancy and transforms the source material to suit the occasion and the time. All that was deemed noble and worthy of memory was pinned on Gilgamesh – a king of the first dynasty in Uruk – by the generations of Babylonians who told his story.

Because the epic is based on undoubtedly much older gynocentric Sumerian material, it is invaluable as evidence of the overthrow of goddess worship and the institutionalisation of the patriarchal ethos 'might is right'. It sheds a great deal of light on Harrison's statement that the Goddess 'who made all things, gods and mortals, is unmade and remade and becomes the plaything of man, his slave, his lure'.[23]

Gilgamesh derives his identity through acts of war and rape. Though his rule is generally oppressive, nature, animals and women bear the brunt of his violence. He is presented as a hero of unbridled aggression and sexual appetite (he leaves 'no son to his father', 'no virgin to her lover') who nevertheless is the 'strong, handsome, and wise shepherd' of the people he oppresses.[24] The once great goddess Ishtar occupies a subordinate position in Uruk: her temple is left 'uncultivated'. The goddess Aruru (another name of the Mother Goddess) is subordinate to the *patron* god of Uruk who orders her to create a strong man to curb Gilgamesh in answer to a plea by the city *fathers*. Thus Enkidu, the 'man-beast', is created.

Enkidu undoubtedly represents a different social order from that of Gilgamesh. He is hairy like an animal, his hair 'sprouts like grain' and looks like a woman's. He 'eats grass with the gazelles', drinks with them at the same watering place and delights in his heart with them. He lives in open country. He is the scourge of hunters, filling their pits, foiling their traps, and in general protecting all animals from the harmful intentions of Gilgamesh's people. It is interesting to note that an armed hunter coming face to face with this peaceful unarmed creature is 'benumbed with fear' at the sight of him, as if to hunt were to break taboo and incur guilt, as if the older law (represented by Enkidu) were still powerful enough to inhibit its violators.

At any rate, in these uncomfortable encounters between the hunter and Enkidu, hunting is singled out as the activity that separates the two social systems. Enkidu's is the non-violent, 'edenic' social order in which humans live in harmony with nature and animals. Nature delights the heart, animals are left undisturbed, women and men look alike. Gilgamesh's social order is based on aggression against animals and separation from nature and it comes about through an open rejection of Ishtar. In other words, the city of Uruk is in a state of political transition and the resulting chaos will abate only through the assimilation of the old order into the new.

Enkidu's role highlights the mechanism of co-optation, whereby the *men* will be encouraged to co-operate with the new rule against their former culture, repudiating their allegiance to the Goddess, women, animals, and the land in exchange for a share in the patriarch's prestige. In the story, Enkidu is taken away from his peaceful existence, his state of a 'man-beast', first by raping a priestess[25] of Ishtar's temple whom the hunter forced upon him with full backing of both Gilgamesh and the hunter's father, then, by tasting the 'strong drink' of men, eating animal flesh, and, ultimately, by partaking of the power and the glory of Gilgamesh as the king's right-hand man. It is clear that hunting, raping, drinking alcohol and eating meat are not natural to the species but are required of men as the conditions of their integration into the 'civilised' (dominant) social order.

The hunt is part of Enkidu's fall from innocence (innocence means 'not noxious, not harmful') and the hunt is related to the primal crime recorded in the Babylonian creation story *Enûma elish*, that is, to the dismemberment of the goddess Ti'âmat by the god Marduk.[26] It is as a hunter that Enkidu joins Gilgamesh in raiding 'the mountain of the cedar, the dwelling place of the gods, the throne-dais' of the Goddess, cutting down the cedar tree sacred to the Goddess and killing the guardian of her sacred forest. And it is Enkidu who insults Ishtar. He 'tore out the right thigh of the bull of heaven and tossed it before her [Ishtar], saying "If only I could get hold of thee, I would do unto thee as unto him; I would tie his entrails to thy side."'

Co-optation and male bonding reinforce a position against a common foe. In the epic, friendship is described as a sharing of power against the Goddess – consequently, against nature and the animals in which she dwells. Bonded in friendship, Enkidu and Gilgamesh mirror each other but, as Virginia Woolf was to point out, male vanity needs female mirrors to reflect men at twice their size. Having absorbed each other's qualities, Gilgamesh and Enkidu ride hand in hand in the streets of Uruk, demanding of the *maids*: 'Who is the most glorious among heroes? Who is the most eminent among men?' The frightened maids have no choice but to answer, now that their Goddess has been humiliated and their priestesses defiled: 'Gilgamesh is the most glorious among heroes. Gilgamesh is the most eminent among men'. The intoxication of victory is short-lived. Ishtar's curse brings death to Enkidu. Grief-stricken, Gilgamesh roams in mourning for his friend and sets out in quest of the plant of immortality. But a serpent 'snatched the plant, sloughing its skin on its return', while Gilgamesh was bathing in a pond. The king then resigns himself to his mortality and, upon his return to Uruk, dedicates himself to strengthening the fortified wall around his city.

The importance of the epic is manifold. Scholars focus on it mostly as source material of the Bible. Man's quest for immortality and his subsequent acceptance of the inevitability of death are seen as the epic's central meaning. To me, the Gilgamesh Epic is a rare document in which the character of Enkidu is the link between the old and the new order, between different ideas of strength and wisdom and between irreconcilable value systems. The epic indicates that worship of the Great Goddess, characteristic of the way of life in 'the open country' (the birthplace of Enkidu), was on the wane in cities such as Uruk as a result of patriarchal oppression. In cities, the position of the Goddess was mainly subordinate and defensive – she punishes Enkidu for his betrayal and her serpent thwarts Gilgamesh's search for immortality. The epic also points to the new gods and kings as solitary in their individualism, their position of high command, power, and lust. The fortified wall around the city works well as a metaphor standing for the paranoia that would develop from such a position and would escalate in time to create the present nuclear arms race which threatens to destroy us all.

Updating Gilgamesh and Goddess murder

Roughly speaking, the values represented by Gilgamesh and Enkidu are similar respectively to those of the European conquerors/invaders/immigrants who came to the American continent, and those of many of the Native tribes they encountered on it.

In 1855 Chief Seattle of the Duwamish tribe was faced with the predicament of having to sell land to the white man or have it taken by force (with guns). He sold. However, he made a speech on this occasion, describing the white man in terms that portrayed him as a modern Gilgamesh: a violent, ruthless hunter who treats the land as if he were God and owned it, a destructive self-destructor whose machines rape the earth, whose noisy cities 'insult the ears' and numb the senses ('like a man dying for many days, he is numb to the stench').

It is a beautiful speech. Even if the style betrays the retouching hand of a white sympathiser, the substance is undoubtedly Seattle's own for it is consistent with all that I have read of Native American writings.[27] His narrative juxtaposes the two cultures and in the excerpts that follow, it is clear that his own is very close to the Earth-oriented value system we could glimpse from the brief account of Enkidu's life before his integration into the dominant order.

How can you buy or sell the sky, the warmth of the land? The idea is strange to us. If you do not own the freshness of the air and the sparkle of the water, how can you buy them from us? . . . Every part of this earth is sacred to my people. Every shining pine needle, every sandy shore, every mist in the dark woods, every clearing and humming insect is holy in the memory and experience of my people. The sap which courses through the trees carries the memories of the red man.

The white man's dead forget the country of their birth when they go walk among the stars. Our dead never forget this beautiful earth, for it is the mother of the red man. We are part of the earth and it is part of us . . .

We know the white man does not understand our ways. One portion of land is the same to him as the next . . . The earth is not his brother, but his enemy, and when he has conquered it, he moves on. He leaves his father's graves behind, and he does not care. He kidnaps the earth from his children. He does not care . . . He treats his mother, the earth, and his brother, the sky, as things to be bought, plundered, sold like sheep or bright beads. His appetite will devour the earth and leave behind only a desert.

The air is precious to the red man, for all things share the same breath – the beasts, the trees, the man, they all share the same breath . . . I have seen a thousand rotting buffaloes on the prairie, left by the white man who shot them from a passing train. I am a savage and I do not understand how the smoking iron horse can be more important than the buffalo that we kill only to stay alive.

What is man without the beasts? If all the beasts were gone, men would die from a great loneliness of spirit. For whatever happens to the beasts, soon happens to man. All things are connected. Whatever befalls the earth, befalls the sons of the earth . . . If men spit upon the ground, they spit upon themselves . . . Man did not weave the web of life; he is merely a strand in it. Whatever he does to the web, he does to himself.

Animistic societies – societies in which everything is endowed with soul – do not strive as we do toward independence from nature, nor do they view nature as a collection of organisms engaged in the 'problem' of staying alive for the benefit of humans. We, on the other hand, no longer think of ourselves as children of Mother Earth but as children of culture and as such we unravel our isolated existence disconnected from 'the beasts' and 'everything that is'. Even so, in Judaeo-Christian cultures where nature is seen as existing solely for humans, the need for mother and our dependence upon her are so strong that we repeatedly deny them by acts of rejection and rebellion, domination and control. Western man maintains his connection to the life force (Mother Nature) through an exercise of power which freezes him in a state of perpetual infantilism. To grow up would mean to acknowledge the source of power and treat all life with egalitarian consideration.

From animal to beast

The dis-enspiriting, un-souling of animals has a political edge that served as an effective weapon in the conquerors' strategies to demolish earth worship. The word 'beast' itself comes from the Sanskrit 'that which is feared' and it is this connotation that gradually passed to the word 'animal', the two being synonymous today. They denote inferior qualities, especially when applied metaphorically to humans: violence, lust, and contemptible, dangerous and 'unnatural' conduct – in short, qualities to be feared in animal and human behaviour alike.

We have seen that Enkidu attacks Ishtar's symbols – the animals he is made to eat, the sacred forest, the bull of heaven – before he threatens the Goddess herself. When a people loses its symbols, it is demoralised and more amenable to manipulation. If sister-animals with which the invaded peoples had identified were despised as beasts, indoctrination into the new order would proceed more effectively. Under these pressures, the invaded/conquered would internalise the negative images of their former 'relatives' and acquire the low self-esteem needed to keep them either integrated in the new order or in bondage.

The serpent is a prime example of this reversal. We read in Jane Harrison:

> The snake among the Greeks was full of *mana*, was intensely sacred, not because as food he supported life, but because he is himself a life-*daimon*, a spirit of generation, even of immortality.[28]

And in Merlin Stone:

> It seems that in some lands all existence began with a serpent. Despite the insistent, perhaps hopeful, assumption that the serpent must have been regarded as a phallic symbol, it appears to have been primarily revered as female in the Near and Middle East and generally linked to wisdom and prophetic counsel rather than fertility and growth as is so often suggested.[29]

The transformation of the serpent from numinous presence (animal) to symbol of evil (beast) makes sense only in a political context. The serpent, which had played a crucial role in so many gynocentric societies over so large a territory, became the focal point of the new mythology and served the 'divide and conquer' policy that strengthened the cult of the patriarch.

Human mortality is a concept introduced by the new gods. Since the serpent had symbolised immortality, it had to be degraded into a despicable beast, hence feared. Thus the Christian God curses it, specifically dividing it from woman and from the bond that held them together.

In Genesis, the serpent appears to Eve from the Tree of Knowledge, which is also the Tree of Life. Eve trusts the serpent ('No! You will not die') and eats the fruit of the forbidden tree. God then forces Eve to break allegiance with her tradition and curses the serpent:

> Be accursed beyond all cattle . . . I will make you enemies of each other: you and the woman, your offspring and her offspring. It will crush your head and you will strike its heel. (Gen. 1: 14–15)

And it worked. In Christian symbology, the Virgin Mary is commonly depicted with her heel crushing the serpent's head. It worked so
well that the fear of snakes is widespread and taken as a given. Some
even believe it to be a kind of atavism inscribed in our brains.[30]

The new gods

Just as the Goddess had the same characteristics the world over, so
the God is similar everywhere. Man, too, named himself through his
gods and took his images with him wherever he went. Woman had
perceived herself as being like unto nature; man named himself as
distinct from nature. The Goddess represented life as it was; the God
represented life as man wanted it to be, celebrating only what he
fashioned with his own hands, from his own will. She had appeared in
her triple aspect, renewing herself in the perpetual life–death cycle;
he appeared alone, fixed for ever in ageless vigour. She had accepted
death as part of life; he was immortal.

For the Goddess, happiness had been a given more in the sense of
wellbeing than ecstatic elation, since it seems to have been the goal of
all her endeavours. This state of wellbeing also is reflected in the
scores of names for the Goddess connected to the ideas of good and
bright. She experienced pain and rage, but only in reaction to harm
done to the mothers by man/god. Conversely, the God did not suffer;
he inflicted pain. He derived his wellbeing from immediate gratifica-
tion of the lust to 'create', administer 'justice', take revenge and rape.
Happiness, man proclaimed through his stories of the God, was earn-
ed, or worse yet, deserved as a reward for obedience to divine law.

Man named himself by an act of separation from and power over
nature, animals and women, ensuring his pre-eminence through
ownership of all. The house (*domus*) and its holdings (*familia*) are
now his to protect and defend. He is lord (*dominus*), he dominates, he
domesticates. This means that nature is no longer treated as a complex of self-regulated organisms under a 'law' of communal kinship
but is brought under *the law* of one king, the single rulers of monar-
chy and monotheism. Responsibility (ability to respond) gives way to
obligation as ethics become arbitrary – functions of will, rather than
principles arising from reality. Thus good and bad give way to standards of right and wrong to which it is politically dangerous not
to conform. Father-rule tears morality out of the fabric of social

conscience which had given mother-rule its cohesiveness and turns it into a political category dictated and policed from the outside, from above. In other words, father-rule destroys the moral relationship with nature characteristic of mother-rule by changing the concept of *nature* into one of *nation* which, like man's holdings (family), needs defence and protection.

The need for war is built into the concept of nation. Unlike nature, which provides a common identity to all that is born of Mother Earth, a nation identifies individuals as isolates by separating them from the group. Individuals are then recombined in unstable aggregates held together by a shared hostility against 'outsiders'. Freud aptly described this state of war when he wrote that 'human life in common is only possible when a majority comes together which is stronger than any separate individual and which remains united against all separate individuals'.[31] The need for communal identity lives on in the human mind but is no longer nourished from inside the organism of the group. Instead, like the new ethics, it is arbitrarily chosen – people rally behind unstable symbols like flags and leaders, ideas and heroes.

Patriarchal gods reflect man's alienation from nature and the group. They are mirror-images of cultures that produced a model of maleness from which the earth and animals were the first to suffer, but which affects all of us in ways counterproductive to wellbeing. In her discussion of the death throes of 'totemistic' thinking, Harrison stressed the dire consequences of the detachment from nature that accompanied the rise of patriarchal gods. She noted regretfully that

the shedding of plant and animal form [by patriarchal gods] marks of course the complete close of anything like totemistic thinking and feeling. It is in many ways a pure loss . . . There are few things uglier than a lack of reverence for animals . . . In art this exclusion of animal and plant life from the cycle of the divine is sometimes claimed as a gain. Rather it leaves a sense of chill and loneliness.[32]

Few people today feel the 'chill and loneliness' of this exclusion, especially among the younger generations conditioned to city environments and mechanical societies. To many of them, nature is 'man's refuse',[33] that is, anything left over from what man cannot use . . . yet. And since nothing prevents anyone from planting a tree and acquiring animals, there is nothing to worry about and environmentalists are getting hysterical about a crisis that does not exist. Man is able to grow things without nature's supportive soil and can feed them with artificial chemicals. He can seed clouds and make rain or snow. He can fuel his body with processed foods and recharge his mind with television and electronic games. He can shuffle genes and breed specific traits in and out of most species, including his own. To those who have staked their futures on these technological 'miracles', nature does not exist except as it is man-made. Thus, the human need to search for and renew the self through private, non-directed and solitary contacts with the earth, *away* from culture, has become a non-search. Mediated one-dimensional images invade homes, offices, automobiles, and possess the individual's mind as they direct, therefore control, thought, speech, 'feelings' and behaviour. In this context, the concept of looking for roots in nature is meaningless.

Alienated, fragmented and possessed, modern man is as rootless as a plant 'grown' in sterile soil – and often just as life-less. Human dependency on nature's processes has been replaced by dependency on man-made, insane products – products developed and manufactured at the cost of plant and animal pain, at the cost of human decency. The new gods of 'our' depersonalised, dehumanised societies are the practitioners and popularisers of reductionistic science and technology – whose 'achievements' are peddled by the media and legitimated in the schools. Re-connecting in kinship to the non-human world around us is the first real step toward saving the earth and *all* species from destruction. But, unless man learns to relinquish his hold on his rationalisations and face the reality of his acts against life, 'closing the circle' – as Barry Commoner has named this reconnection – will remain an ecologist's dream. A culture that defines adulthood in terms of one's ability to separate from mother/ nature and defines mental health according to the smoothness of this separation, is a culture that denies its life-blood. Such a culture's relationship to self and nature is bound to be destructive.

Notes

1. Although they characterise 'primitive' languages, holophrases are not to be confused with the early stages of children's speech, which some psycholinguists call holophrastic. See David McNeill, *The Acquisition of Language: The Study of Developmental Psycholinguistics* (New York: Harper & Row, 1970).

2. Quoted in Peter Matthiesson, 'Stop the go road', *Audubon*, 81 (1) (January 1979), p.62. The Yurok, the Karok, the Tolowa, and the Hupa tribes regard one group of isolated peaks and rocks in the Blue Creek wilderness of the Siskiyou as a sacred 'High Country'. Consequently, they oppose the construction of highways in this sacred place.

3. Jane Ellen Harrison, *Epilegomena to the Study of Greek Religion* (New York: University Books, 1966; Cambridge: Cambridge University Press, 1921), p.475.

4. For a living example of the difficulties encountered in such attempts, see Christa Wolf, *Patterns of Childhood*, translated by Ursule Molinaro and Hedwig Rappolt (New York: Farrar, Straus & Giroux, Inc., 1980), and *Cassandra*, translated by Jan van Heurck (New York: Farrar, Straus & Giroux, Inc., 1984; London: Virago, 1984).

5. Merlin Stone, *When God Was a Woman* (New York: Harcourt Brace Jovanovich, 1978), p.18.

6. Anne Cameron, *Daughters of Copper Woman* (Vancouver: Press Gang Publishers, 1981; London: The Women's Press, 1984), preface.

7. In our language, abstract words tend to represent absolutes. Thus, 'egalitarianism' conjures up all kinds of myths. Human experience is largely a matter of order that necessitates the assignment of one's 'place' in the social organisation, therefore the 'class system' has always existed. However, there is an immense difference between what I would call the lateral stratification found in matriarchal societies and the pyramidal structure that characterises patriarchy. The former arises out of the needs of the community as a whole from a recognition of 'specialness' and differences that have intrinsic survival value. It allows great flexibility and, above all, it is not predicated on the need of one individual to debase another in order to enhance himself. Words like 'slave' and 'nobility' as we understand them today (oppressed/oppressor) are meaningless in this context.

8. For a discussion of the absorption of the Triple Goddess into various trinities of gods, see Mary Daly, *Gyn/Ecology: The Metaethics of Radical Feminism* (Boston: Beacon Press, 1978; London: The Women's Press, 1979), pp.75–79.

9. It is interesting to note that round male figures like the Buddha are not looked upon as symbols of fertility but of spiritual fulfilment. These

30 *Rape of the Wild*

interpretations reflect polarised gender stereotypes: woman creates through her body; man creates through the intellect. The damage to woman of the polarisation is in the restriction of her creativity to reproduction, which precludes all other creative activity of which she is eminently capable. Moreover, to represent 'spiritual fulfilment' by roundness of the belly strongly suggests womb envy. The Greeks were more straightforward in their acknowledgment of womb envy. Although they did not name it as such, they invented a god-figure (Zeus) capable of 'giving birth' to full-grown 'children' *from his body* (Athena from his brow, Dionysus from his thigh).

10. Harrison was working in a male-dominated field and her concessions to male 'authority' are sometimes quite obvious and annoying. It must have taken enormous courage to present her evidence in support of a theory that had no currency at the time.

11. The serpent is the unmistakable associate of the goddess throughout the East. For sharp analyses of its *non*phallic, numinous import see Stone, *When God Was a Woman*, pp.198-214 and Jane Ellen Harrison, *Themis: A Study of the Social Origins of Greek Religion* (London: Merlin Press, 1977), pp.270-1 and *passim*.

12. ibid., p.168.

13. See the back cover of the paperback version of Richard E. Leakey and Roger Lewin, *Origins* (New York: E.P. Dutton, 1979; London: Macdonald & Jane's, 1979) for these three blurbs attributed to John Pfeiffer in *Psychology Today*, to *Library Journal*, and to *Time Magazine*, respectively.

14. For a discussion of the hunter theory of evolution and the evidence used to support it, see Chapter 2.

15. Leakey and Lewin, *Origins*, p.233.

16. Cameron, *Daughters of Copper Woman*, p.97.

17. Stone, *When God Was a Woman*, p.71.

18. Conversation with Diana Eck, Boston, Massachusetts, 31 August 1979.

19. Carolyn Merchant in *The Death of Nature: Woman, Ecology and the Scientific Revolution* (San Francisco, California: Harper & Row, 1980; London: Wildwood House, 1982) traces the break with nature to the rise of scientific thought in seventeenth-century Europe.

20. Lewis Thomas, *The Lives of a Cell: Notes of a Biology Watcher* (New York: Bantam Books, Inc., 1974), pp.154-5.

21. ibid., p.152. This may be true for scientific words, although the mental predispositions that prod the scientist to refine tools in answer to a 'need' are inseparable from the language in which he *thinks* this tool, and inseparable as well from the word he will choose to name his new gadget.

22. Louise B. Young, *Earth's Aura* (New York: Avon Books, 1979), p.80.

23. Jane Ellen Harrison, *Prolegomena to the Study of Greek Religion*, 3rd edn (Cambridge: Cambridge University Press, 1922), p.51.

24. All quotes from the Gilgamesh Epic are taken from Alexander Heidel (trans.), *The Gilgamesh Epic and Old Testament Parallels* (Chicago, Illinois: University of Chicago Press, 1949).

25. See Stone, *When God Was a Woman*, pp.xx and 156 for a discussion of the common practice in male scholarship translating words referring to the 'holy women' or the 'sanctified women' of the temple as 'prostitutes' or 'courtesans'.

26. Alexander Heidel (trans.), *The Babylonian Genesis: The Story of Creation* (Chicago, Illinois: University of Chicago Press, 1951), pp.40-1.

27. The same sensitivity and synchrony with Earth are manifest in the recent words of Brooke Medicine Eagle when she commented on her vision which would guide her in her work as a healer. 'For healing to come about, we need to honor the spirit within ourselves and within all things. The earth is our mother; we must take care of her.' See Steven S.H. McFadden, 'Warriors of the rainbow', *Sanctuary*, 25 (1) (October 1985), pp.15-16. All quotes from Chief Seattle are taken from a transcript of a television programme presented by The Human Dimension and aired in Pittsburgh, Pennsylvania, winter 1972. The narration of that programme was adapted from a speech by Chief Seattle of the Duwamish tribe, Washington Territory in 1855.

28. Harrison, *Themis: A Study of the Social Origins of Greek Religion*, p.271.

29. Stone, *When God Was a Woman*, p.199.

30. Carl Sagan writes, 'The implacable mutual hostility between man and dragon, as exemplified in the myth of St George, is the strongest in the West . . . But it is not a Western anomaly. It is a world-wide phenomenon.' See *The Dragons of Eden: Speculations on the Evolution of Human Intelligence* (New York: Random House, 1977; London: Hodder & Stoughton, 1978), p.150.

31. Sigmund Freud, *Civilization and its Discontents*, trans. and ed. by James Strachey (New York: W.W. Norton & Company, Inc., 1962; London: Hogarth Press, 1963), p.42. Compare Jane Ellen Harrison: 'We are still too apt to put the cart before the horse, to think of the group as made up of an aggregate of individuals rather than of the individuals as a gradual segregation of the group.' See *Epilegomena to the Study of Greek Religion*, p.470. Individualism in the sense of integrity (whole-ness) – the integrity of human groups *and* animals, animals *and* plants, plants *and* the earth, the earth *and* the heavens held together by indivisible bonds of kinship – this type of individualism is incompatible with the patriarchal notion of individualism as an isolated member of the group

whose integrity is broken. For only as man became antagonistic to nature did he separate himself from her and proclaim the sovereignty of 'I'. The louder the rhetoric of individualism, the less real it is in practice.

32. Harrison, *Epilegomena to the Study of Greek Religion*, pp.449-50.

33. This comment was made by a student during a class discussion at Brandeis University, Waltham, Massachusetts, spring 1982.

2. Shots in the dark

Every creature is better alive than dead, men and
moose and pine trees, and he who understands it
aright will rather preserve its life than destroy it.

Henry David Thoreau, *The Maine Woods*

Man is not a natural species: he is a historical
development.

Simone de Beauvoir, *The Second Sex*

Movers of culture: hunters

Man has become an expert at rationalising his destructiveness. There
are instances of the hunting and killing of nature and animals from
which many reasonable men, not completely alienated from their
feelings, would turn away in horror and disgust. But when violence is
presented under the guise of a 'noble purpose', all kinds of abuses go
unrecognised and often are even praised. Such is the fiction
surrounding the hunt.

While it is preposterous to single out one activity from the totality
of human experience and interpret it as the prime mover of culture,
hunting – man's oldest profession – has been given that dubious
honour. According to current anthropological theory, hunting is 'the
master integrating pattern of culture',[1] it is 'the crucible in which
natural selection pounded at the grist for the human spirit as well as
the human body'.[2] In this view, *Homo sapiens* is a natural predator

whose hunting activities account for the achievements of civilisation. Without it we would be no further than the ape.

Such theorising is puzzling to those who do not subscribe to the inevitability of violence and male domination which are implicit in it. The belief that 'our intellect, interests, emotions and basic social life'[3] have been formed by the experience of the hunt contains a basic error. The use of the pronoun 'our' lumps together women and men of all cultures and of all times in an activity that commonly has been attributed to males only and which other scholars have demonstrated to have been far from universal. In addition, such speculation ignores all anthropological data which would show that survival relied more heavily on the skills necessary for the gathering and consumption of vegetable food than on the killing of animals and the eating of meat.[4]

Given the frequency with which men wage wars and commit violent crimes, proponents of the hunter theory of evolution would have been more credible if they had limited themselves to their observation that 'men enjoy hunting and killing'.[5] For it is not *hunting* that formed our intellect, emotions, etc., but rather those hunters who, finding pleasure in the hunt, abandoned the ancient rituals of atonement that had accompanied the killing of animals for food. Thus, *some* hunters in *some* parts of the world developed a form of power based on the model of hunting. These hunter–kings spread their value systems through the violence of wars, destroying nature, killing animals, raping women and in general abusing those they enslaved. It is in this context that human intellect, interests, emotions, and basic social life evolved in patriarchy.

By glorifying the hunt as a major evolutionary step, many social scientists justify a culture of brutality toward and rape of all that is viewed as 'fair game'. Moreover, hunting as a sport serves as the paradigm activity in which the re-enactment of the hunt and the kill reinforces the normalisation of a violent act. By playing hunter, man ritualises what he sees as his greatest glory: his passage from ape to human and the consequent creation of a category of domination, the politics of which have changed the face of the earth and the quality of our lives.

If theorists can argue that man is linked inevitably by his own evolutionary process to hunting/killing/violence, then man may be absolved of responsibility for his violent culture in which nature is perceived as fair game, as the rightful object of his predatory inclinations. For this reason it is necessary to review the hunter theory of evolution, to challenge its assumptions and understand its implications for all those who fall under the category of prey in patriarchy. The hunter theory of human evolution was first formulated in the early 1900s. In the wake of Darwin and Freud, Raymond Dart suggested that violence was the factor differentiating man from other primates. By violence he meant the calculated killing of animals, whether the kill was used as a source of food or not. Since then Dart's successors have added elaborate qualifiers but the theory remains essentially unchanged. That is, that through the co-operation and increased intellectual activity demanded of the successful hunter, the groundwork for the emergence of *Homo sapiens* was laid.

Weapons

Of particular importance to this theory is the dating of tools, most commonly interpreted by scholars as weapons. The farther back such implements can be dated as instruments of violence the more credibility is gained with respect to man's immersion in a hunting culture. Furthermore, the more remote the find in terms of time, the more conjecture is required to give meaning to these tools, with less opportunity for confirmation and more possiblity for control.[6]

Palaeoanthropologists and archaeologists disagree considerably in the dating of early 'tool' manufacture. As they shuffle years by the millions, we do not know on whose hairy chest to pin the honour of having started us on the road to culture. However, according to them, a hairy chest it undoubtedly was, even though it is thought that women were the gatherers of fruit, nuts and leafy things for which they fashioned *agricultural* tools, and this well *before* man took to hunting. Still the scholars insist that although the presapient hominid was making spectacular adjustments to the new environment caused by changes in climate and the heavings of a turbulent earth, it did not become fully human until it dawned on the male that he could flake stones and kill large animals and that he could either eat the carcass or leave it to rot on the ground.

According to Jacques Bordaz, a specialist in the classification of 'tools' (read 'weapons') from the Pleistocene Epoch, 'man could now [300,000 to 400,000 years ago] range widely and securely in small bands to better exploit plants and animal resources.'[7] Archaeologist R.E. Leakey, son of the famous Mary and Louis Leakey who dated modern man's appearance in Africa at a still controverted two to three million years, writes that *Homo erectus* 'were people *in tune* with their environment, exploiting every part of the plant and animal kingdoms [*sic*] the season of the year dictated' (emphasis added).[8] Louis Leakey carried his fascination with early 'tools' to the point of experimenting with them, i.e. killing animals, presumably to test the efficacy of early man's technology in exploiting his environment. Thus, acts that culminate in the wounding to death of sentient creatures are interpreted as manifestations of man's harmony ('in tune') with his environment, his 'tools' being the crucial invention which enabled him 'better' to exploit the earth.

Division of labour

The shift from a gathering to a hunting culture did in fact have enormous consequences for the development of the human species. What can and must be argued is whether that development was beneficial. As R.E. Leakey has observed, there is a correlation between the increasing importance of meat in the diet and the increasing dominance of men over women.[9] Justification for this dominance is to be found in what functions as the cornerstone to the theory of evolution which glorifies the hunt: the division of labour between the sexes. With this division, the prototype of man as active and woman as passive is sealed in a time frame that began hundreds of thousands of years ago.

With the killing of large animals and the consequent 'division of labour' (read 'dominance of male over female'), it is believed that cultural evolution 'began overtaking genetics as the major determinant of human behaviour'.[10] Anthropologist John Pfeiffer could draw this odd conclusion because to him, as well as to all enthusiasts of the hunt, hunting created new situations which strained the brain, causing man to invent co-operative strategies and a language with which to communicate them to fellow hunters. Therefore, male hominids developed larger brains to accommodate these new functions and females developed a wider pelvis to accommodate large-brained offspring. Few have described this situation more naïvely than Pfeiffer, for whom larger brains created 'a fundamental problem in the design of the body, a problem involving the optimum dimensions of the female pelvis'.[11] He goes on to say:

> From a strictly engineering point of view, the obvious way of allowing for the delivery of bigger-brained infants is to enlarge the pelvic opening and widen the hips, and evolutionary pressures were at work which favored this solution. The difficulty is that individuals with wider hips and related modifications lose a measure of mobility. As far as speed is concerned, the ideal pelvis is a male pelvis. Women cannot generally run as fast as men, a disadvantage in prehistoric times when flight was called for frequently.[12]

Thus females, no longer able to run with the males, grew increasingly dependent on them for protection against 'predators' and for the spoils of men's hunting expeditions.

According to Pfeiffer, hunting also brought about a sexual revolution for man, for 'he [*sic*] [became] independent of one great natural rhythm, the internal rhythm of oestrus' and thus 'it became possible to select the time and the place for intercourse'.[13] As psychologist Joyce Contrucci exclaimed: 'This is a slick, educated way to say that the female lost control of her own sexuality!'[14] In this new social arrangement, women could be raped at the whim of the male who 'selected the time and the place', especially if she could not run as fast as he could. She is perceived by him as available. In short, like the animals he allegedly hunted, she had become fair game.[15]

The hunt accomplished what its rationalisers want to justify, and that is the dependence of women on men for food and protection – a crippling dependence which is defined and accepted as 'natural' in patriarchal culture. Thus, students in introductory psychology courses read:

> Until recently in human history it probably was to everyone's advantage for males to act masculine and females to act feminine. In the primitive societies . . . survival depended on a division of labor between the sexes. The women, bearing and nursing one child after another, could not roam far from home. The men were free to range far and wide hunting for animals to provide food. Moreover the men, being physically stronger, protected the home against wild beasts and unfriendly strangers. The tradition was established early and served a purpose. Women were dependent. Men were dominant.[16]

Violence

There is, it seems, no end to the wonders of the hunt. Man's 'progress', born of a violent act and culminating in the domination of one sex of one species over the entire world population of living creatures, led men to the killing of other men, i.e. to war and manslaughter.

But not all local populations of australopithecines made and used tools [weapons] and it is likely that only a few effectively made the transition to tool use and then went on to displace or destroy other local populations of australopithecines that had not achieved an equal degree of cultural [*sic*] evolution.[17]

Supposedly this 'effective transition' was accomplished through man's 'aggressive' drive which theoretically is fixed in the brain ('prewired' – a term which likens the brain to a computer) or in the genes (phylogenetically programmed). In either case, we are told that man's violence and his domination of nature, animals and women are inevitable and pivotal in the achievements of civilisation. (It is interesting to note that warring is considered a mark of *superior* cultural evolution. Over 2,000 years ago, Aristotle had rationalised the justice of war with the same reasoning. Wars were necessary to secure slaves (people *born* inferior) and good soldiers acquired their skills by practising on animals (hunting).)

Paul MacLean, former chief of the Laboratory of Brain Evolution and Behavior at the National Institute of Mental Health (Poolesville, Maryland) has located the bio-sociological origin of violence ('aggression') in the reptilian brain – a knot-like affair swaddled in layers of neocortex that have accrued upon it in the course of evolution. Being the oldest part of the human brain, this supposedly is the seat of inborn impulses or instincts which account for man's intolerance, territoriality, 'incessant struggle for position and domination', hierarchical social organisations as well as the violence man uses to achieve his social arrangements and goals.[18]

Assuming that the reptilian brain plays such a crucial role in violent behaviour, what happens to the notion that women are naturally passive? Do we lack a reptilian brain in the same way as men lack a complete X chromosome? If intolerance, territorial struggle and violence are a function of the neural circuitry of an arcane part of the human brain, how can one explain the historical and present existence of human societies which strive for peaceful coexistence, which retreat into inaccessible areas when invaded, which do not encourage power needs or project masculine images of bravery and violence?[19] Has their 'prefrontal neocortex . . . the mental stuff of which we imagine angels are made'[20] been on a faster developmental track than that of the rest of humanity? Have their reptilian brains atrophied? What has 'gone wrong' with them? Such wide differences in social behaviours and social arrangements place MacLean's 'findings' on shaky ground. They are too neat and self-serving to be real.

According to ethologist Konrad Lorenz, man's 'aggression' is a carry-over of his animal origins but, unlike other animals, man lacks the phylogenetically programmed inhibitory mechanisms to check the hunting skills he acquired suddenly at some point in prehistory. What Lorenz fails to explain is why, in the whole animal queendom, man is so uniquely imperfect as to lack the inhibitory mechanisms with which other animals are born. Lorenz claims that man's killing problem is exacerbated by the anonymity and the physical–emotional detachment afforded him by artificial and remote-control weapons. He noted that 'no sane man would even go rabbit hunting for pleasure if the necessity of killing his prey with natural weapons brought home to him the full, emotional realization of what he is actually doing.'[21] Clearly 'natural weapons' are hands. Hands pick up stones, spears, high-powered rifles, etc. with which man kills his prey for pleasure, and these hands are directed by a conscious human brain. The problem is precisely the fact that there can be no full, emotional realisation, regardless of the kind of weapons used, when one can perceive a sentient creature as object (prey). The underlying emotional detachment/deadness allows for the process of objectification which is at the base of the hunting syndrome.

The solution, then, is to make 'the best' of a bad situation. Lorenz suggests 'dangerous undertakings, like polar expeditions and, above all, the exploration of space' in which nations could 'fight each other in hard and dangerous competition without engendering national or political hatred'.[22] Such solutions reflect the mentality of violence and domination that are so much a part of a rapist culture. They are instances of rape of the wild where nature again is objectified, probed, used, and brought under control of man's futile attempt to redirect his 'aggression' to 'better' ends. Of course, these theorists do not consider such attempts as futile. They construe what is actually violence as progress, and continued violation of the integrity of being as achievement. In this sense, ethologist Richard Dawkins believes that 'modern *man*' has outgrown his prehistoric past and has the ability to modify not only his environment but his genetically programmed behaviour.[23] Now that 'we' have acquired enough knowledge of ourselves, 'we' can control those destructive traits that brought us to the brink of extinction.

And yet, looking at the direction of science, reading about men's futuristic visions, we see more and more control exercised by fewer and fewer individuals over the many, through cybernetics, mood and behaviour control, pre-natal genetic and memory alterations. These 'achievements', together with the nuclear and chemical threats to the environment, the robotisation of work, the desensitisation to life, the chemicalisation of foodstuffs, the proliferation of iatrogenic diseases, the extinction of animals and plant species, the increasing rigidity of the political structure, the impoverishment of imaginative life – all give reason to think that if this represents the optimum in 'human' evolution, the hunters who are shaping it are insane.

Movers of culture: gatherers

As Virginia Woolf has said, though we see the same world, we see it through different eyes. We have seen the world too long through the eyes of man. Women have been taught his version of the past, and have been indoctrinated with his values, the values of the hunting state. Yet it is likely that gathering was the prime mover of culture until the 'battle of the sexes' occurred which revolutionised society. The transition from mother-right to father-right took thousands of years and was accomplished with more or less thoroughness according to the size and strength of the matriarchies scattered throughout the world. Before then, it is probable that groups of females and males engaged in day-to-day living, expanding their ties with nature. The division of humans along sex lines became real, therefore important, only at the time when one sex sought supremacy over the other – a time that began with the killing of animals sacred to the Goddess and the debasement of Mother Earth.

It is easy to fall into a romanticisation of the remote past and imagine social realities that fit one's vision of a good life. Many archaeologists have done this. Their reconstructions of prehistory are based on the most fragmentary evidence – some splintered bones, a few teeth, and what seems to be an abundance of worked stones (called 'tools') scattered throughout the world. They wax eloquent on what may have been our origins even while admitting that their schemes are 'a complete fairy tale, a fabric of *more* or *less inspired* guesses' (emphasis added).[24] But a guess – inspired or not – leaves open the possibility of other 'guesses', other possible explanations for the interpretation of gathered facts and observations. Guesses become valid theories when they are viewed as plausible enough to be accepted by the community of scholars. Therefore it is not difficult to see that when this community is predominantly comprised of those in power, theories substantiating their position in society would gain more favour than those suggesting a differing view. One can also see that the more threatening the alternative is to the status quo, the more emphatic the rejection or, as in the case of the idea of women as movers of culture, the more it is simply overlooked/ignored/dismissed.

By denying validity or even recognition to alternative interpretations, access to alternative values and beliefs capable of freeing a society from its own self-destruction is closed. Thus 'guesses' become theories and 'theories' become self-serving dogmas when proposed in a closed system of thought. The interpretations given to archaeological/anthropological finds must be seen for what they are: 'explanations conceived in the light of individual belief'.[25] Thus it is not surprising that the finds of archaeologist James Mellaart, at Catal Hüyük, Turkey, which revealed the existence of a homesite of gynocentric settlements dating back at least 10,000 years,[26] were minimised. Despite the finding of 'tools', Goddess figures and religious objects that would support Mellaart's theory of a society organised around the primacy of the female, cultural anthropologists selectively tell us of the 'polished obsidian mirrors found at Catal Hüyük which were presumably an early reflection [*sic*] of female vanity'.[27] Although in keeping with patriarchal propaganda about women, this comment hardly 'reflects' the nature of the real women who built and shaped this highly evolved community. What can be seen in the polished mirrors of Catal Hüyük is just how much of *our* prehistoric past remains buried. It is important for women to remember that man's theories are guesses – explanations that suit his nature and support his state. Likewise it is important to remember that women's guesses are theories capable of offering interpretations of the past that reflect our values, our beliefs and the significance of our lives.

An envisioning

As a vision and a dream, matriarchies have exercised the imagination of many seekers of more benevolent and reasonable alternatives. Even a cursory acquaintance with many so-called primitive contemporary societies as well as with archaeological sites and prehistoric artefacts lends credence to the historicity of matriarchies which is still denied by obdurate and fearful scholars.

By matriarchies I do not mean the matrilineal cultures recognised by all anthropologists. These groups, where they still exist, have been largely contaminated by the white man's presence. They are used to justify the hunting theory of culture because they show a division of labour along sex lines even though anthropologist Margaret Mead has observed that when tribal men leave the settlement for the ostensible purpose of hunting, they end up more often than not under a tree shooting nothing more than the breeze.[28] Robert Graves caricatured matriarchies as the state in which 'women were the dominant sex and men their frightened victims.'[29] Most probably, the notion of dominance itself rose with the establishment of the supremacy of males as lords of the household. In a genuine matriarchy women are the makers of major decisions in all spheres of activity, not merely as determiners of descent, nor as cooks, nor victims of constant pregnancies.

The existence of matriarchies throughout the world indicates that different groups of people at the same time *can* organise around different human experiences and values and develop divergent cultures. In the distant past, warmongers seem to have lived near more peaceful people whom they eventually swallowed in warfare. Matriarchies most likely suffered this fate.

Specifically, one species of *Australopithecus* disappeared some 500,000 years ago and the Neanderthals vanished between 10,000 and 13,000 years ago. Scientists accept the view that both were exterminated by their violent relatives (Cro-Magnons) who had a superior technology. Carl Sagan speculates that the brains of Neanderthals and Cro-Magnons the two branches of *Homo sapiens* – evolved along different lines, which led the superior Cro-Magnon 'to destroy utterly our husky and intelligent cousins'.[30] John Pfeiffer states that the Neanderthals 'had no chance against these people and these institutions'.[31]

As their burial sites and animal cults suggest, the Neanderthals possessed a high degree of religious consciousness. They had a culture advanced enough to have produced many of the famous animal cave paintings in Spain and Southern France. Some say that they were not killed by wars but as a result of being 'too specialised', that is, too well adapted biologically and behaviourally to the harsh climate of ice-gripped Europe to survive in warmer weather.[32] Others suggest that since *sapiens Neanderthalis* occupied most of the world, they survived and continued to evolve whenever climatic conditions allowed. In some cases, they even 'married' into tribes of *sapiens sapiens* (Cro-Magnons), especially in the Near East.[33]

Reality is in the mind's eye. I like to think of Neanderthals as the originators of those matriarchal traditions that persisted so strongly through the Middle East into historical times and which make it reasonable to speculate that the physical, psychological and social developments attributed to man's profession, hunting, could easily have developed from woman's profession, gathering. Instead of weapons, many artefacts of our remote past could as easily have been ingenious edible-root diggers and mashers, nut crackers, slicers, implements to gather wood for the hearth and shelter.

If a large brain is the result of exercise – thinking, imagining, communicating mind-stretching experiences – the deliberate gathering of food, whether this involved the sporadic capture and killing of small animals or not, is likely to have precipitated the development of the brain as well as hand dexterity. The acquisition and transmission of information about the edibility, the nutritional and medicinal properties of plants combined with information about their location and growth habits, require an active use of memory, intelligence, language, and the manufacture of *tools* (utensils) to gather, handle, store and prepare them.

Social cohesiveness is more likely to have arisen from the mother–infant bond and the need both to protect and feed the young than from male bonding developed on occasional hunting trips into the woods. Collective nurturing and the play element involved in the caring of the young is likely to create a language rich in emotional nuances and a vocabulary far more imaginative, complex, and affective than the language derived from the hunt, in which there is no trust, no affection, only thrill. The gathering and preparing of food as well as the care of infants require an infinity of observations and judgments crucial to wellbeing. With time to think and time to dream I see thoughts of connectedness gradually emerging that would form the creation stories that later would become ritualised into worship. Practical and aesthetic concerns such as the weaving of cloth, blending of colours and shaping of matter (clay, wood, stone) would turn into technology and art. I see congeniality and sharing. It is not coincidental that the word 'company' means the eating of bread together (Latin: *com pane*, with bread). If sharing meat had been as vital as some scholars would have us think, we would have a word to reflect that reality. The sharing of meat comes to us associated with sacrifice, not company.

There are many examples of the patriarchal bias in interpretations of archaeological/anthropological finds. When confronted with piles of animal bones such as those of elephants, horses, rhinos, and so on, which died 300,000 years ago in what used to be a swamp in Torralba, Spain, I would think of the flight of animals before a natural forest fire, and their tragic death there, mired, unable to escape. I would *not* think of 'spectacular hunting expeditions' or of men lighting fires in the bush to 'stampede their prey'. The fact that the site of this massive animal death also contains 'acheulian tools' (hand axes that look like grain thrashers) suggests that humans lived there, not necessarily that men drove these animals to the swamp, killed them, and ran on abandoning their 'tools'.

The remains of some fifty elephants at Ambrona, Spain, could be a communal grave, since elephants feeling death impending travel long distances to die where other elephants have died and others still will come to die. Or again, a natural disaster could have killed the herd all at once. It takes a hunting mentality to imagine that men slaughtered fifty elephants at one time. To construct an analogy with today's pygmies who delight in elephant hunts is bound to be vitiated by the fact that today's pygmies have had contact with the white man's greed for ivory. Knowing the price he will pay for tusks certainly is part of that delight. Moreover, comparisons between contemporary hunter-gatherer tribes and tribes of *Homo erectus* living 300,000 years ago do not take into account the changes that occur with the passing of time. Pygmy culture today is different from what it was in the past.

Another case in point is the hut in Soviet Moldavia, one wall of which is built of mammoth skulls, tusks and shoulder blades. These bony remnants are just as likely to have been supplied by natural events as by mass hunting, the current popular explanation. As the Ice Age progressed, there were movements of glaciers, melting and freezing over of ice sheets, and changes in the flora and fauna everywhere, particularly around the ice sheets. The mammoth did not survive the warming of climates and the changes in vegetation. It is plausible that a band of humans would chance upon a few dead mammoths already decayed and would thus take advantage of the bones, using them as raw material to build their shelters. This does not mean that men did not hunt mammoths – they too had to keep warm, they too had to eat during those turbulent times. It means simply that to kill for survival does not entail mass slaughter.

I like to think of women as movers of culture. In Western culture, we are traditionally said to be conservative, meaning opposed to progress. In general we oppose all that is destructive of us and what we love. We do not believe the rationalisations given us by those who see gain in destruction. For example, we oppose territorial expansion because it means the death of sons, the rape of daughters, the wounding of land, the general abuse of those not directly involved in combat (the civilians), and general destruction of all that is dear to us.

Thus women are not seen as playing an important role in the evolutionary path that led the hominids forward into humanhood. We are not opposed to progress as such, but our notion of progress is more ecological, therefore conservative in the sense used today by conservationists. Whenever we have succeeded in keeping a sense of ourselves as separate and different from the cultural model of femininity, whenever we have been able to assert our values and nonconformity without feeling that we are melting into nothingness, we have been, and are, basically and universally lovers of life. And it is this loving I see as prime mover of culture.

The kind of alternative theorising I have done here concerning our remote past is not only appealing and plausible, it is vital. It is vital because in the process of women imagining our own history lies the possibility of discovering our own values, and in those values lies our hope for the future.

Man's oldest profession

I have no sympathy for hunters. Their habit repels me as being senselessly brutal. Their language embarrasses me as sounding piteously immature. They remind me of irresponsible little boys driven to savagery out of boredom, a boredom so desperate that relief comes only from the thrill of hunting that culminates in the kill. Quite simply, hunters need to be 'turned on' to life. One of them expressed his inability to respond to nature unless he controlled/killed it when he said to me, 'Walking in the woods doesn't turn me on unless there's a purpose to it. Marking trees. Shooting deer. That's really living.' This middle-aged man, well-off, respectable-looking, and soft-spoken, makes a living from house-hunting, that is, from real estate, which he finds very dull. Hunting becomes the fix that enables the hunter to bear the humdrum of his unfeeling existence as a cog in the wheel of culture.

However my purpose is not to understand hunters but to situate hunting in the culture that spawned it. Hunting is the *modus operandi* of patriarchal societies on all levels of life – to support one level is to support them all. However innocuous the language may sound – we hunt everything from houses to jobs to heads – it reveals a cultural mentality so accustomed to predation that it horrifies only when it threatens to kill us all, as in the case of nuclear weapons. Underlying all this hunting is a mechanism that identifies/names the prey, stalks it, competes for it, and is intent on getting the first shot at it. This is blatantly done when the prey is named woman,[34] animal, or land but it extends to whatever phobia happens to seize and obsess a nation, whether this be another nation or a race other than that of power-holding groups.

Nature has been blamed for being either seductive (and dangerous) or indifferent to man. Siren-like, she beckons and invites hooks and guns in the same way women are said to lure men and ask for rape. Or, like the cold, uncaring 'bitch', nature does not respond to man's plight and must therefore be punished. Seduction and indifference are in the mind of the beholder who projects them in order to rationalise his acts and the rationalisation works because the culture approves it. We know that women want to be raped as much as deer and lions want to be shot and the earth, sea, and skies are asking to be gouged, polluted, and probed. But ever since God said we had all been created to submit to man's will, it has been legitimate to objectify women, animals, and nature, attributing to them characteristics and behaviours which say a great deal about the patriarch's state of mind and nothing about us.

Sadomasochism: the 'insurmountable problem'

To perceive something alive as an object is part of the sadomasochistic syndrome Pulitzer prize winner Ernest Becker sees as the *creative* and *heroic* solution to the 'insurmountable problem' life itself presents to man. In *The Denial of Death*, Becker names 'the problem' as nothing more than having to live with a body subject to the natural laws of limitation and death. Thus, he is forced to live in terror of meaninglessness and compelled repeatedly to perform acts of brutality in order to survive. Those who cannot accept to be a *part* of the life-cycle must live in the realm of sadomasochistic fantasy and seek self-actualisation in violence. Blaming nature for one's limitations (one's animality) is like blaming mother for being born and hating both for one's inability to cope with life. Thus Becker projects this hatred on to nature by calling it callously unconcerned, 'even viciously antagonistic to human meanings', and not surprisingly finds a callously vicious solution in flagrant perverse acts against life which 'compel nature to defer' and raise him above it. Indeed *this* is the essence of hunting. It is an exercise of power on the part of one who feels overwhelmed, fragmented and frightened and it explains the pathetic urge to kill anything bold enough to be alive.

The real significance of a philosophy such as Becker's is that it articulates the sadomasochism to be found in every aspect of a culture that leads us shamelessly to exploit the body of nature and name that exploitation 'transcendence', 'progress'. (It is interesting that Becker received a national award and that many critics praised his 'courageous' exploration of man's existential dilemma, which was simply an exacerbation of the old body/mind dualism.) A tradition that encourages us to free our bodies from the limitations of nature is one that plucks us from the web of life, leaving us stranded and longing for the very biophilic connections we are taught to repudiate. Blind to the inherent contradictions and delusions, man splits reality into discrete, self-contained and antagonistic categories – nature/culture, body/mind, emotion/reason – claims them all and calls himself healthy, whole and sound of mind. He is unruffled about the fact that he 'loves' animals, joins conservation societies, rescues abandoned dogs and cats *and at the same time* sinks hooks into fish and fires bullets into 'game', shoots rodents who occasionally munch vegetables in his backyard, condones the clubbing of baby seals to death, and the infliction of injury and excruciating pain on laboratory animals, hits rabbits, squirrels, hedgehogs, skunks, opossums by the thousands as they cross his highways, leaving them to their fate and, in an all-out war against 'the enemies of mankind', seeks to exterminate all manner of insects and 'lesser' life forms that threaten his comfort and possessions. It is the rare man who sees these acts as contradictions. He is even more rare who experiences them as conflicts. Such contradiction and delusion are cornerstones of the romantic tradition – a tradition which urbanely conveys sadomasochism into the realm of 'normal' human feelings and relationships by masking the brutality of 'love' grounded in the objectification of the 'love object'.

The hunt romanticised

In simple terms, romanticism is a function of the idealisation process whereby brown paper is turned into holiday wrapping. A romantic removes the 'love object' from the reality of its being to the secret places of his mind and establishes a relationship of power/domination over it. There can be no reciprocity, no element of mutuality between the romantic lover and the 'love object'. The quest (chase) is all that matters as it provides a heightened sense of being through the exercise of power. Romantics engage in sadomasochistic games with their victims played against a background of obstacles, potentially threatening situations, and grandiose schemes. Since one cannot sustain the frenzy of feeling resulting from pursuit of an ideal – by definition, inaccessible – the romantic game point is death. The hunt, as epitomised in the idealisation of the chase, of the kill, of the hunter and of his victim, is the mainstay of romanticism.

Romantic images of the hunter and the hunt abound in the arts and the media. An example of the unexamined contradictions and delusions that sustain such romanticisations can be seen in the words of the eminent art historian Sir Kenneth Clark, who described the medieval institution of the hunt in *Animals and Men*, a work commissioned for the benefit of the World Wildlife Fund.

Hunting was considered a festive occasion, in which the pursuit and death of a few animals was of little importance compared to the pleasure it gave to a quantity of human beings, and there arose the much quoted paradox that hunters are the only men who really love animals.[35]

Hunting – festive – pursuit – death – animals – pleasure – human beings – hunters – love. Certainly an odd string of associations that would confound a reader with a life-loving mentality.

Elsewhere in the book appears a representation of Paolo Uccello's painting, *Hunt in the Forest*, which depicts deer surrounded by placid-looking men with weapons, dogs and horses, about to pounce upon the deer from all sides. (This image is echoed in a scene in Ingmar Bergman's film *The Virgin Spring* in which a young girl blended with the landscape in much the same way as Uccello's deer and, as in Uccello's painting, was unaware of the two repulsive men who were lying in wait in the thicket before attacking and raping her.) According to Clark, in Uccello's painting 'there is no hint of brutality or death . . . Here the union of man and nature comes curiously close to the image of the Golden Age.'[36] Through the lens of the romantic the tension of the brutality about to overwhelm the deer is lost as we are asked to see instead images of man's communing with nature and the harmony of a Golden Age.

Clark goes on to comment on a painting by Lukas Cranach in which animals are being massacred a few feet away from a family enjoying an outing on the river, the members of which – including the child's pet dog – are all oblivious to it. The contrast between the brutality of the hunt and the frivolous indifference of the well-to-do boaters enjoying private violin music should increase the horror toward hunters and boaters alike. (One could compare *this* image with a scene in the film *Cabaret*, in which a group of bourgeois Germans complacently enjoy a lavish meal while Nazis are harassing and viciously terrorising people in the street nearby.) However, to Clark, 'Up to modern times it was conventional to enjoy it [the chase] and a spectacle such as that depicted by Lukas Cranach would have given nothing but pleasure to most normal men and women.'[37] Here brutality as a norm is excused as something of the past and, in the name of art, is disconnected from the overall pattern of destructiveness that pervades this culture. The norm determines the normality of men and women. When the norm is destructive, normal men and women destroy whether they engage in the hunt, as Cranach's hunters, or, like his boaters, 'enjoy' themselves while violence is going on around them, or, like the viewers to whom Clark alludes, take pleasure from Cranach's spectacle.

The efforts of modern man to rationalise the contradictions and delusions surrounding the hunt and the hunter extend to the romanticised images he fashions of primitive man as the archetypal hunter with the hunt as the *sine qua non* of his existence. These images are inferred, in part, from primitive cave paintings which depict animal and human figures. Very different images of our [*sic*] remote past and pastimes occurred to me after regarding many textbook representations of the actual primitive portraits.

In primitive art, cave paintings portray a direct relationship between the artist and the animal *as* animal. In fact, the animal itself, not the hunt and not the hunter, is the focal point of cave art. In those rare instances in which the animal is represented as wounded, the 'hunter' can be inferred but is not seen. In addition, the animal is drawn not as prey or victim, but as self-contained energy so unusually lifelike and beautiful that art historians agree in attributing deep religious motivation to the artists who drew them. The primitive artist who emerges for me from these cave paintings is one who is in tune with the *life* of the animal and whose spirituality en-souls/animates the visual representations.[38]

In contrast, modern portraits of the archetypal hunter/hunt share one common characteristic: the animal is used as a projection screen for man's repressed and thwarted feelings, that is, the animal symbolises something other than what it essentially is. It serves to highlight the hunter's power, prestige, etc. It is invariably prey to the hunter who occupies centre stage. The animal is thoroughly objectified and brutality is presented as heroism.

In the main, these portraits run the gamut of vulgarity. For example, a supermarket in Waltham, Massachusetts, has a decorated wall above its meat department with three 'painted' hunting scenes. An Eskimo spears a seal, a Native American is about to dispatch an arrow into a buffalo, and an African thrusts a javelin into a lion, next to the caption 'Your violent struggle for food is over. On these premises is your happy hunting ground.' Underneath this mural, real and ordinary people buy 'cuts' of meat dissociated from the animal and from the slaughterhouse (the 'hunting ground'). The message conveyed by the caption is a lie. Food is a 'struggle' created by over-population and consumerism rooted in an economy of waste. Thus the 'violent struggle' for food is *not* over; it is either disguised or displaced. Disguised, in that the white man kills anonymously, behind the scenes. Displaced, in that the struggle is in the animal's psyche –

unseen, unheard, and unspoken for. It must 'live' through the brutal negation of its needs in pens too small. It is fed poisonous chemicals that deform its body as they accelerate its growth. In addition, for the food shopper, the 'struggle' has shifted from physical to economic stress – people having to hunt jobs in order to afford the psychic pain of the animals they eat. Indeed, it is not just animal flesh that the shopper purchases in those plastic-wrapped packages but the psychic struggle of the once-living animal.

Another particularly disturbing contradiction, with attendant delusions, blurred by romanticisation is the phenomenon of the artist–hunter, who kills then draws or paints his victims. The artist–hunter loves nature – birds, animals – but without the exchange, the mutuality that would indicate a perception of the other as a self. If there were such mutuality, there would be no such person as an artist–hunter. The life and work of the Swedish naturalist Bruno Liljefors provide clear examples of the neurosis underlying such 'love' of nature. As a child, Liljefors is said to have lain awake at night devising 'schemes for trapping birds, eager to hold and study them up close'. His first weapon was the bow and arrow, but, because he could not get close enough to his quarry he 'inevitably graduated to the gun'. Still dissatisfied, he took up stone throwing and 'as he skinned and mounted his triumphs, he drew and studied their anatomy'.[39]

After describing Liljefors as an ardent lover of nature, Don R. Eckelberry speculates that Liljefors' obsession with hunting 'may have been psychologically rooted in admiration for the contest of power between the hunter and the hunted growing out of his childhood weaknesses'.[40] Regardless of the early personal experiences that may or may not have fed the obsession, it certainly is a strange admiration that seeks and triumphs in the death of the beloved.[41]

The reverse side of Liljefors' killing problem is his identification with helpless animals. 'He could . . . be just as sentimental as those he criticised, nursing injured and orphaned animals and going out of his way to protect an imperiled nest with young. He was moved when a frightened fox cub crawled into his shirt for protection.'[42] This description provides clues to the sadomasochistic character of the artist–hunter and to the delusional mechanisms enabling one without conflict to perceive the self and be perceived by others as both a lover and killer of animals. Publication of romanticised renditions of the life and work of the artist–hunter by major conservation groups such as the Audubon Society provides the ultimate fiat and camouflage for the irreconcilable duality of love expressed by killing.

From the romantic to the real

Hunters often pose as conservationists who love nature, giving rise to yet another contradiction comfortably entrenched in this culture. In point of fact, hunters do not love nature as such but rather how they feel *in* nature as they stalk and kill her animals. Dependent for their thrills upon what nature 'provides', they therefore spend a considerable amount of money to ensure that conservation lands as well as fish and animal preserves are regularly stocked. They return compulsively to woods and lakes, rivers and fields, marshes and oceans, to live through the power of their rods and guns.

When rigorously challenged as to the morality of their predilections, hunters commonly resort to rationalisations that disguise their self-interest as 'concern' for animals and for other people. For example, 'deer would starve to death if hunters did not cull the herds', or 'bears would cause too much damage if not kept in check by hunters'. The deer's main natural predator is the wolf which hunters all but exterminated. As for marauding bears, it is human overpopulation and the 'need' to industrialise that is causing an expansion of *suburbia* into the 'wilderness', taxing the earth and all that lives on it. Thousands of innocent wild animals are forced from *their* habitats and then blamed and exterminated for damage *they* cause to human settlements. The deer did well when it was left alone. So did the bear.

Perhaps from the animal's point of view it is immaterial whether it is killed by the claws of a bear or by the bullet of a hunter. But it makes an enormous difference to the continuation and *quality* of life whether human beings kill like the bear or like the hunter. Bears do not kill gratuitously for 'pleasure', status, profit, power, masculinity. Hunters do. Bears kill because they have to eat what they kill in order to survive. The overwhelming majority of the 20.6 million 'registered' hunters in the United States do not kill for survival. Bears kill the weak. Hunters take the biggest and the best. Bears give back to the earth. Hunters give back nothing.

After he had witnessed a moose hunt, Henry David Thoreau wrote:

This afternoon had suggested to me how base and coarse are the motives which commonly carry men into the wilderness. The explorers and lumberers generally are hirelings, paid so much a day for their labor, and as such they have no more love for wild nature than woodsawyers have for forests.[43]

Thoreau's experience of that hunt brought home to him the uniqueness of life, the rare and beautiful quality that is felt only by participating in 'the perfect success' of every part of nature. In other words, every part of nature is a gift in itself. For Thoreau the capacity to know the heart of the pine without cutting into it is to love the healing spirit of the wild without killing it. This contemplative, non-utilitarian, non-materialistic love of nature often passes as romantic because it is emotional and appears to ignore such realities of life as building houses and keeping warm. Thoreau's own attempt at self-sufficiency – for which he had to cut timber – did not prevent him from participating as fully as he could in the mystery of the wild.

Participation in nature is in diametric opposition to the romantic appetite for nature epitomised in the hunt, an appetite which consumes the object of its love and which is insatiable because based upon a neurotic need for power and control. Participation in nature is based upon a recognition of the reality that nature exists of, for, and by herself; that she is ordered by principles and forces which defy manipulation and harnessing; and that understanding of nature flows from the experience of her and not from the experiment upon her, from being with, not being over her. Participation in nature joins the lover and the loved in regenerative, mutually sustaining cycles of living and dying.

Notes

1. William S. Laughlin, 'Hunting: an integrating biobehavior system and its evolutionary importance', in *Man the Hunter*, edited by Richard B. Lee and Irven De Vore (Chicago, Illinois: Aldine Publishing Company, 1968), p.319.
2. Melvin Konner quoted in Philip Zaleski, 'Of Archaeopteryx, the ! Kung San, and Dendrite Spines', *Harvard Magazine*, 85 (1) (September–October 1982), p.39.

3. Sherwood L. Washburn and C.S. Lancaster, 'The evolution of hunting', in *Man the Hunter*, edited by Lee and De Vore, p.293.
4. See Sally Slocum, 'Woman the gatherer: male bias in anthropology', in *Toward an Anthropology of Women*, edited by Rayna R. Reiter (New York: Monthly Review Press, 1975), pp.36–50, for an example of an 'early' effort by feminist scholars to expose the male bias in anthropological theories and to provide evidence and argument for the importance of gathering in early hominid survival and evolution.
5. Washburn and Lancaster, 'The evolution of hunting', p.299.
6. In this connection I am reminded of the party slogan of the totalitarian state in George Orwell's *1984* (New York: Signet Classic, 1961, p.32; Harmondsworth: Penguin Books, 1970): 'Who controls the past controls the future: who controls the present controls the past.'
7. Jacques Bordaz, *The Tools of the Old and New Stone Age* (New York: Natural History Press, 1970; Newton Abbot: David & Charles, 1971), p.38.
8. Richard E. Leakey and Roger Lewin, *Origins* (New York: E.P. Dutton, 1979; London: Macdonald & Jane's, 1979), p.133.
9. ibid., p.233.
10. John E. Pfeiffer, *The Emergence of Man* (New York: Harper & Row, 1969; London: Thomas Nelson, 1970), p.13.
11. ibid., pp.137.
12. ibid., pp.137–8.
13. ibid., pp.147 and 142.
14. Conversation, Norwell, Massachusetts, January 1981.
15. Pfeiffer carries the division of labour theory even further with one of his inimitable sleights of hand that eliminates women from prehistory. He writes that by 10,000 BC the *world* population is estimated at 10 million. Of these 10 million, 100 per cent were hunters. He wrote this after he had taken great pains to establish that hunting was for males only.
16. Jerome Kagan and Ernest Havemann, *Psychology: An Introduction*, 4th edn (New York: Harcourt Brace Jovanovich, 1980), p.391.
17. Gerald Berreman *et al.*, contributing consultants, *Anthropology Today* (Del Mar, California: Communications Research Machines, Inc., 1971), p.169.
18. Mary Long, 'Ritual and deceit', *Science Digest* (November/December 1980), pp.86–91, 121.
19. These characteristics common to peaceful human societies were described by G. Gover, 'Man has no "killer" instinct' in M.F.A. Montagu (ed.), *Man and Aggression* (New York: Oxford University Press, 1968) and reported in Kay Deaux and Lawrence S. Wrightsman, *Social Psychology in the 80s*, 4th edn (Monterey: Brooks/Cole, 1984), pp.208–9.

20. Mary Long, 'Ritual and deceit', p.121.
21. Konrad Lorenz, *On Aggression*, translated by Marjorie Kerr Wilson (New York: Harcourt, Brace & World, Inc., 1966; London: Methuen, 1966), p.242.
22. ibid., p.282.
23. Richard Dawkins, *The Selfish Gene* (Oxford: Oxford University Press, 1976), p.215.
24. Leakey and Lewin, *Origins*, p.117.
25. *Webster's Seventh New Collegiate Dictionary* (Springfield, Massachusetts: G. & C. Merriam Company, 1967).
26. This date is conservative since there are structures on lower levels yet to be excavated which point to more archaic times. See James Mellaart, *Catal Hüyük: A Neolithic Town in Anatolia* (New York: McGraw Hill, 1967).
27. Roger M. Keesing and Felix M. Keesing, *New Perspectives in Cultural Anthropology* (New York: Holt, Rinehart & Winston, 1971), p.97.
28. Margaret Mead, lecture delivered at Regis College, Weston, Massachusetts, 1972.
29. Robert Graves, *The Greek Myths*, vol. I (Baltimore, Maryland: Penguin Books, Inc., 1955; Harmondsworth: Penguin Books, 1969), 1.1.
30. Carl Sagan, *The Dragons of Eden: Speculations on the Evolution of Human Intelligence* (New York: Random House, 1977; London: Hodder & Stoughton, 1978), p.107.
31. Pfeiffer, *The Emergence of Man*, p.203.
32. Leakey and Lewin, *Origins*, p.125.
33. Elizabeth Fisher offers a fascinating review of this thought-provoking theory in *Woman's Creation* (New York: Anchor Press/Doubleday, 1979; London: Wildwood House, 1980), pp.132–4.
34. The predictable inclusion of women in the ranks of man's rightful prey is easily seen in the fur industry which is keen on maintaining the connection between hunting, fur animals and women. Its advertisements degrade women because they invariably fuse animals and women in the same identity of prey, an identity that appeals to the hunter in man and the victim in woman. These ads tell the woman to take the bait (the fur coat) that will apparently bring the man to her feet. In reality she is the prey being brought down. She and the fur animal – one 'alive' and the other dead – are one and the same. After looking at dozens of these images it became obvious to me that the advertisers address not so much the woman who is lured into wearing the fur as the man whose money will buy it. Even when man does not actually hunt animals, his success is still reflected in the kill.
35. Kenneth Clark, *Animals and Men* (New York: William Morrow, 1977; London: Thames & Hudson, 1977), p.57.

36. ibid., p.211.
37. ibid., p.208.
38. We do not even know whether the artists were women or men, although most art historians refer to them in the masculine gender. In view of collective identity of tribal people, cave art is likely to be the result of collective work over several generations rather than the boasting of an individual hunter about the day's kill.
39. Martha Hill, 'Liljefors of Sweden: the peerless eye', *Audubon*, 80 (5) (September 1978), p.81.
40. Don R. Eckelberry, 'Of animals and art', *Audubon*, 80 (5) (September 1978), p.105.
41. I can still admire the bird paintings of J.J. Audubon and Bruno Liljefors; they are indeed beautiful. Then I think of the birds and animals freshly shot to enable the artist to reproduce their likenesses. The cost of my pleasure is too high. I am morally outraged with Martha Hill when she uncritically writes (op. cit., p.104) that 'the paintings of John James Audubon, Wilhem Kuhnert, and Carl Rungius were enhanced by the detailed knowledge of morphology gained from freshly shot animals'. The *lives* of the animals so freshly shot were not enhanced by their killers' romantic passion.
42. ibid., p.104.
43. Henry David Thoreau, *The Maine Woods* (New York: Thomas Y. Crowell Co., 1961), pp.156-7.

3. Animal experimentation

These things that, by his science and technology,
man has brought about on this earth, on which he
first appeared as a feeble animal organism . . . these
things do not only sound like a fairy tale, they are an
actual fulfilment of every – or almost every – fairy-
tale wish.

Sigmund Freud, *Civilization and its Discontents*

I can imagine cages more sour to the spirit
than the arbor rising on this island:
the cage that studies the experimental subject,
the cage that is committed to the pet,
the cage that demands survival of the endangered,
the cage that rehabilitates the disobedient and the mad,
the portable cage of nightmare . . .

Robin Morgan, 'Voices from six tapestries',
'Taste: The Monkey Speaks'

. . . that doctor don't know what he talking about. He
must never seed no mare foal. Who say they don't
have no pain? Just 'cause she don't cry? 'Cause she
can't say it, they think it ain't there? If they looks in
her eyes and see them eyeballs lolling back, see the
sorrowful look, they'd know.

Toni Morrison, *The Bluest Eye*

Living tools: the animals

Animals used in laboratory research are living tools. I take the expression 'living tool' from Aristotle, who applied it to the slave's situation in the master's world. The slave deserves unequal treatment, he said, 'for there is nothing in common to the two parties; the slave is a living tool and the tool a lifeless slave.'[1] Naming the slave a tool enables the master to ignore and/or deny the slave's experience of slavery. It enables him to objectify the slave, to be objective about slavery.

In Aristotelian logic, slaves are naturally inferior because they lack the ability to reason, therefore they are objectified as things subjected to and dependent upon the master's control. Since there is no common ground between them, the master need not scruple about how he treats the slave. Since slaves are tools, their only function is to extend the master's capabilities and help him do what he cannot do on his own.

With respect to laboratory animals, objectifying them as tools used to further the interest of Science enables the experimenter to remain emotionally detached and to ignore and/or deny the animal's experience. Experimental psychologist Clark L. Hull aptly described this situation when he said that objectivity in animal research consists of regarding 'the behaving organism as a completely self-manipulated robot, constructed of materials as unlike ourselves as may be'.[2] As Andrea Dworkin put it, objectivity is what does not happen to you.

From this perspective, the researcher strips the animal of its natural attributes and manipulates it to suit his design. The animal no longer exudes grace, strength and health. Restricted in body and mind, and drastically altered, it is afflicted with physical and mental diseases. The researcher does not identify with, feel connected to, this animal. Rather he coolly observes and measures its reactions to the substances and conditions to which he subjects it. As the animal is forcibly alienated from its essence and isolated from its kin, so it is separated from the researcher and, by virtue of the violence the researcher does to animal integrity, he alienates himself from his own nature and from the root of humanity.

In societies such as Aristotle's and our own, in which the sense of commonality between all living things has been broken and lost, societies fractured and stratified by brute force/power, there *is* nothing in common between experimenter and animal. Our culture teaches us that we are separated from animals by differences in our respective degrees of sentience and intelligence and that, as animals are naturally inferior to humans, we are entitled to patronise and use them as we see fit.

Several decades after Hull gave his directive to would-be animal experimenters, W. Lane-Petter struck the familiar theme of 'animal-as-inferior; animal-as-living-tool' when he spelled out in his preface to *Animals for Research* the ethics he hoped would guide the use of animals in laboratories: 'An experimental animal – and this applies above all to highly defined strains and types of mice and rats – is part instrument, part reagent, a complicated and *incidentally sentient system*' (emphasis added).[3]

Just how 'incidental' the sentience of animals is to many experimenters is clear when one reviews the work of men such as Robert White of Case Western Reserve University and the Cleveland Metropolitan General Hospital. His achievements include removing the brains of monkeys and dogs and preserving them alive, grafting a brain on the throat of a living dog, and transplanting the heads of rats and monkeys onto the bodies of decapitated rats and monkeys, keeping the heads alive for days.[4] According to White: 'Our main purpose is to offer a living laboratory tool: a monkey "model" in which and by which we can design new operative techniques for the brain.'[5]

Many other people, lay and professional alike, would agree with medical doctor John C. Lilly, the renegade brain researcher who conducted most of his later experiments on dolphins, when he said that 'the lowest-grade human moron is above the highest genius in the gorilla or chimpanzee clan'.[6] Lilly's criterion for this quaint gradation of intelligence is the size of the brain.

> In certain cases it is necessary to dehumanize the animal and not confuse his purpose with ours. With this point of view I agree *as long as the brain is very much smaller than ours.* This is the way to strike pay dirt in research with small-brained animals. I spent many years working with cats and monkeys and found this point of view a very good one to take with them. It is most profitable from the standpoint of obtaining rapid results.[7]
> (Lilly's emphasis)

Relative brain size has also been used as an argument to justify racism and sexism, blacks and women alike having been characterised as having smaller brains than their oppressors. Dehumanisation always 'strikes pay dirt' for those who choose to use and abuse others.

The rationale for using animals in research has not changed since Claude Bernard (1813–78), who fathered biochemistry on the bodies of large dogs, first formulated it as follows: it 'consists in never practising on a man an experiment which would only cause him harm in any degree, even if the result would greatly interest science, that is to say, [would benefit] the health of other men' (my translation).[8] Behind laboratory walls all over the world, Science (men and women paid for their scientific work) drills, incises, chips, injects, inserts, cauterises, lesions, sutures, amputates, paralyses, tests, deprives, rewards, jabs, and shocks legions of living creatures which are more often than not fully conscious, i.e. not under anaesthesia and postoperative sedation. All this is done in 'the interest of Science' and to 'benefit the health of men'. The picture varies according to time, place, and the nature of the experiment – sometimes the researcher is more 'sensitive' than at others, guidelines stricter, sanitary conditions better, and so on. Such measures may affect some aspects of the lives of the animals, but the fact remains that those lives are being violated.

There is no pain

'Living tools', 'animated instrument' (as Ivan Pavlov named one of his experimental dogs), 'behaving organisms' 'robots' and the abbreviation 'Ss' for subjects[9] are words and phrases designed to erase the animal's experience. That experience is pain. Researchers go to great lengths to avoid naming it, even when they purposely set out to study pain. To look at pain without naming it is to objectify pain, to transmute it into a category of knowledge. Thus detached from the subjective experience of the animal, pain can be observed and measured as, for instance, the rate of contractions of guinea pig intestine to a particular stimulus. But pain is not a corporeal entity. It is a perceptual phenomenon that involves a creature's nerve-endings and brain in an intricate, subjective interplay. And pain is pain, whether the 'subject' is a victim of misogyny, racial hatred, or speciesism.

In the handful of examples that follow and that are chosen from among the abundant documentation of animal research, it is quite clear that animal pain and the researcher's drive for power are at the core of experimentation.

Claude Bernard, whom I mentioned earlier, was described *admiringly* by a contemporary who saw him at work in his 'laboratory', a narrow, damp corridor, in which he stood 'before his animal table, his tall hat on, his long grey hair dangling down, a muffler about his neck, his fingers in the abdomen of a large dog which was howling mournfully'.[10] (It is interesting to note that the harm Bernard inflicted on his animals so horrified his wife that she tried in vain to stop him. In the end, she separated from him and contributed lavish sums of money to humane societies in an effort to counteract the effects of his work.) The large dog of today, when not anaesthetised, is sometimes 'prepared' by laboratory attendants who strap it to a table and remove its vocal cords. No noise. No pain.

Ivan Pavlov and his colleagues spent over a quarter of a century investigating 'the activities of the cerebral hemispheres in the dog'. They discovered the conditionability of the salivary reflex that made Pavlov's name famous. To read *Conditioned Reflexes*, the compilation of his lectures/demonstrations delivered in 1924 at the Military Medical Academy in Petrograd, is to experience the nightmare of his dogs, although there is never so much as a hint that the dogs suffered, sometimes atrociously, from Pavlov's progressive sadism. In fact, Pavlov thought it appropriate to reassure his audience that his dogs did *not* suffer. His experiments might upset 'very sensitive people' but this was unjustified, according to him, for he had *measured* no appreciable changes in the pulse or in the respiration of the animals he subjected to strong stimuli. It was in one of these lectures that Pavlov spoke of his 'remarkable' dog who had ten different conditioned reflexes, earning him his nickname of 'animated instrument'.

It is not uncommon to find experimenters like Pavlov who want to continue to enjoy and to profit from the pain they inflict on animals. Pavlov won the Nobel prize for literally driving his dogs mad and torturing them. *Conditioned Reflexes* cites no less than 236 published studies conducted on 'man's best friend' in his laboratory. Of this research, he could only say that he needed more such 'studies', for in 1924 'after having acquired some knowledge . . . we feel surrounded, nay crushed, by the mass of details, all calling for elucidation'.[11]

Pavlov continued his experimentation, advancing in fame and funding while exonerating himself from responsibility for the pain he caused and actually blaming his victims for suffering. For example, one of Pavlov's dogs was unfortunately intelligent enough to understand what was happening to her, as well as having the will to resist him, his laboratory apparatus, and procedures. Finally coerced into 'acceptance', *she* was faulted for her pain.

> She slinks along behind the experimenter on the way to the experimental rooms, always with her tail between her legs. On meeting members of the staff, some of whom constantly try to make friends with her and pet her she invariably and quickly dodges them, draws back and squats down on the floor. She reacts in the same manner to every slightly quicker movement or slightly louder word of her master, *and behaves toward all of us as if we were her most dangerous enemies from whom she constantly and most severely suffered.*[12] (emphasis added)

This passage will sound all too familiar to women who have had the courage to recognise male power as the source of their oppression and to name it. In a system in which violence and hostility toward women are normalised, the woman who resists the violation of herself, who will not be led to submit to male power or patronisation – which is a disguised form of violence – is precisely the woman men (and some women) will criticise and devalue the most. She is 'angry with men'. She is the 'man-hater'. She is 'paranoid'. She behaves toward men 'as if [they] were her most dangerous enemies from whom she constantly and most severely suffered'. Thus, her sanity as well as her veracity are denied. Like Pavlov's dog, though she speaks out, she is silenced.

Pain perception was the focus of Ronald Melzack and T.H. Scott's classic study on social isolation in dogs. Under the auspices of the Rockefeller Foundation, the Foundations Fund for Research in Psychiatry and the National Research Council of Canada, they restricted Scottish terriers from puppyhood to maturity in individual cages specifically designed to deprive the dogs of sensory and social experiences. They then proceeded to observe and measure the dogs' pathological reactions to their manipulations.

Melzack and Scott used strong electric shock and burning, i.e. they struck matches and attempted to push the flame into the dogs' noses. 'To the astonishment of the observers, seven of the ten restricted dogs made no attempt to get away from *E* [the experimenter] during stimulation . . . and *E* was able to touch [the noses of four dogs] with the flame as often as he wished.'[13] Not satisfied with burning, they tried jabbing the dogs' skin with needles, still presumably to measure the *dogs'* pathology. 'While the dog was held at the neck, a long dissecting needle was jabbed into the skin at the sides and hind thighs about three to four times'.[14] The dogs raised in non-restricted environments reacted violently to these painful assaults. However,

> *E* was often able to pierce the skin of [the restricted] dog completely so that the needle was lodged in it without eliciting withdrawal or any behavioral indication that pain was being 'felt' or responded to other than spasmodic, reflexive jerks. [When released, the dogs stayed close to *E*] who was then able to repeat the procedure and jab with the needle as often as he wished.[15]

Melzack and Scott have shown through animal torture what torturers throughout history have known all along: it is possible to traumatise the sense out of living creatures and bring them to the point at which they submit to any atrocity without a whimper while becoming hopelessly dependent upon their torturers. The professed astonishment manifested by the authors of the above cited passages is as gratuitous as it is hypocritical. To devise these methods is madness. To apply them 'as often as one wishes' is sadism. To publish them as legitimate scientific activities and to fund them as ways to elucidate the healing of damaged minds (psychiatry) is the institutionalisation of cruelty.

None the less, the *Es* spared themselves the realisation that their actions are morally repulsive by ignoring the animals' experiences and justifying the omission/distortion as scientific objectivity. Thus Melzack and Scott were able to conclude: 'Indeed, to say that these restricted dogs perceived fire and pin-pricks as *threatening*, or even as painful in any *normal* sense, would be anthropomorphism rather than inference from observed behavior.'[16] In the context of the *Es'* violence, the word 'normal' sounds strangely out of place. As for anthropomorphism, to be accused of it in the slightest degree is to be discredited as a scientist. It means the researcher is not being objective. It may mean that one has slipped into seeing a connection between oneself and the animal subject. It may mean that one is beginning to *feel* that the 'behaving organism' is not constructed of materials so 'unlike oneself'. To attribute human-like feelings to animals would actually be the beginning of wisdom. As Joan McIntyre has written:

'We would not be harmed by returning to the roots which once nourished us, which still, unseen, link together all life that lives, and feels, and thinks, and dies, on this, our common planet.'[17] To feel this interconnectedness is a scientific taboo – totally ridiculous and unprofessional. To not feel it is to set the stage for sadism.

The acts of animal experimenters such as Bernard, Pavlov, Melzack and Scott are not qualitatively different from those which the infamous Marquis de Sade committed on his victims. In her brilliant analysis of pornography, Andrea Dworkin devotes a lengthy essay to de Sade which ought to silence the many who continue to romanticise *him* as a victim of a puritanical society. She discusses, among other things, de Sade's treatment of Rose Keller. In 1768, de Sade took Rose Keller to a dark room in his house and locked her in. An hour later, he returned and told her to undress. 'She refused. He tore her clothes off, threw her face down onto a couch, tied her arms and legs with ropes. He whipped her brutally.' He cut her with a knife, rubbed wax and brandy in the wounds as well as 'an ointment that he had invented. . . . Later, Sade alleged that he had paid Keller to be whipped so that he could test his ointment.'[18]

De Sade rationalised his brutality to women in the same way as experimenters rationalise their cruelty to animals – their acts fall within the cultural norm as defined by men. 'I am guilty of nothing more than simple libertinage such as is practised by all men more or less according to their natural temperaments and tendencies.'[19] Dworkin points out that the modern fascination with de Sade resides in the fact that his sexual obsessions are both forbidden and common, and that, like many men, he held the use of women as his absolute right.

Absolute right. Common practice. Blaming the victim. All go hand in hand in justifying the sadism of animal research as well as the sadism of male sexual violence. In a way reminiscent of Pavlov's experiments with 'animated instruments' and the subsequent 'mass of details' calling for 'elucidation' – i.e. more violation of animals in research – rapists justify rape by first perceiving women as 'living tools' placed on the earth by their god to gratify the desires of men. They violate her and claim that she 'asked for it'. Rape trials, during which the victim is forced to relive the horror of her violation, are the setting for the accumulation of the crushing 'mass of details' that call for elucidation, not of the rapist's mentality, but of the *victim's*. Blaming the victim ensures the continuation of rape. The New

Bedford, Massachusetts gang rape trial (1984) is a case in point. In addition to the crushing mass of details surrounding the victim's alleged participation in the crime against her, rape, as violence against women, was further obscured and both court and public attention further directed away from the rapists' acts by charges of racism brought against the defence.

Research such as that of Paul MacLean, who invades the brains of monkeys in pursuit of the seat of human sexual aggression, also ensures the continuation of rape.[20] Pinioned in special chairs with electrode grids permanently cemented to their skulls, male monkeys are forced to expose their brains to MacLean's 'millimeter by millimeter' probing, presumably to elucidate human sexual pathologies. A description of his 'findings' and interpretation is worth quoting at some length.

> In the dorsal hypothalamus area just above the focal region in the hypothalamus involved in agonistic (fighting) behavior, stimulation elicits full erection usually accompanied by vocalization. Then as the electrode is lowered a little further, signs of angry or fearful behavior begin to appear, as indicated by the quality of vocalization, struggling, biting, and showing of fangs. Afterwards there is characteristically a rebound erection. At the point where the pallihypothalamic tract loops over the medial aspect of the fornix, only agonistic signs are elicited. Finally as the electrode leaves this focal area stimulation primarily evokes biting or chewing. *The findings would seem to throw some light on the neural basis for aggressive and violent expressions of sexual behavior.*[21] (emphasis added)

It needs to be stressed that 'violent sexual behavior' (rape, that is, from the perspective of the victim) is a problem of human males and certainly not a problem of monkeys. This type of violating research actually serves as a legitimation of rape, first by the violation of the animals who, once trapped in man's laboratory, are entirely at the mercy of their tormentors. In addition, the statement that there is a 'neural basis' for rape suggests it is 'natural' to man and that there is nothing he can do about it. Attention is redirected from the actual victim of rape to the perpetrators of rape who are cast as hapless victims of their brain circuitry. Furthermore, the suggestion that rape 'resides in the brain' leads to the conclusion that attempts to control it would involve invasions of man's brain, while leaving man's misogynistic, power-based culture intact. The invasion of another creature's brain is simply another form of rape.

Another conclusion drawn from this line of research conducted in MacLean's laboratory is that since the head and tail are in physical proximity in the limbic lobe of the brain, oral sexuality is normal. The resulting 'enhancement of life' is that now psychiatrists are able to help 'relieve guilt feelings in a number of their patients about oral-sexual fantasies and related behaviors'.[22]

No animal, large or small, has evolved biologically and psychically to be used as a living tool; to fulfil its destiny in tanks and cages, strapped to experimental chairs and tables; to further man's causes and help him devise ways to cure his mental and physical disorders. Disease and neuroses are human problems. Progress is a human obsession. No animal has played a role in these disorders. No animal is responsible for them. And no amount of animal research will correct them.

Through the eyes of the dead

> [The scientist] does not wish to see with the lively,
> wayward eye of the artist, which allows itself to be
> seduced by what is charming, dramatic or
> awesome – and to remain there, entranced. It seeks a
> neutral eye, an impersonal eye . . . in effect, the eyes
> of the dead wherein reality is reflected without
> emotional distortion.
>
> Theodore Roszak, *Where the Wasteland Ends*

The real function of the 'animal-as-living-tool' is to provide the researcher with a crutch whereby he can achieve the patriarchal ideal of godliness: power to 'create', power to destroy, power to control. Freud saw this relationship between imperfect man and his science, his vehicle to perfection, when he said:

> Today [man] has come very close to the attainment of [his] ideal, he has almost become God himself . . . Man has, as it were, become a kind of prosthetic God. When he puts on all his auxiliary organs he is truly magnificent . . . Future ages will bring with them new and probably unimaginably great advances . . . and will increase man's likeness to God still more.[23]

At about the same time as Freud was writing these words in *Civilization and its Discontents*, Spanish histologist Ramon y Cajal expressed the same sentiment about man's science being the springboard to his greatness. 'Knowledge of the physiochemical basis of memory, feelings, and reason would make man the true master of creation. His most transcendental accomplishment would be the conquering of his own brain.'[24] In 1970, French biologist Jean Rostand anticipated man's successful efforts to clone life when he expressed an idea similar to Freud's original comment.

> By causing life to be born, for the second time, of something other than itself, man will have closed the great, mysterious cycle. A product of life, he will have in turn become a producer of life. He will have come a little closer to the image he formed of God.[25]

To achieve these 'godly' goals, scientists must not only be highly technically trained, they must also be emotionally dead, for it is by violating and destroying untold numbers of animals that their so-called 'mastery of creation' is wrought. Those scientists who have not lost all of their ability to recognise and respect the life of other sentient creatures, are painfully aware of this requirement as they train for their professions. As one physician of my acquaintance put it, her class was taught that 'work' on animals was necessary 'to teach us desensitisation', meaning the detachment necessary 'to avoid being overwhelmed by the horror of certain things'. Another physician described the animal experiments she had to perform as part of her training as 'profligate, non-creative, redundant, time-wasting, life-wasting, dehumanising'. Yet, she did them. She convinced herself that she was silly for feeling upset since no one else seemed to be bothered. Certainly, no one objected.

One such 'classical experiment for medical students' is described by José Delgado in *Physical Control of the Mind*. The exercise is to

> anesthetize a rabbit or other small mammal and to expose its brain in order to stimulate the motor cortex . . . students are generally impressed by seeing the movements of an animal placed under the command of a human being. The demonstration is far more elegant if the experimental animal is completely awake and equipped with electrodes implanted in the brain.[26]

What impresses me about this 'demonstration' is that medical students are not *horrified* on seeing another living creature jump like a puppet on a string at their command. The desire to conform is especially strong for those at the bottom of the power hierarchy seeking their way to the top. Accordingly, very few students of science have the courage and integrity to question their teachers about the morality of 'working on' animals. They know that being 'squeamish', 'emotional', 'uncooperative', and critical would jeopardise their careers. Yet most likely, most of these students have already lost the ability to connect in kinship with animals long before entering professional training establishments. As undergraduates, they refined what they had begun to learn in school, that is, to suppress feelings for animals in the laboratory/classroom while 'loving' their pet animals at home. When those students finish professional training, their ability to compartmentalise is complete. By then, most have learned to look upon animals, and indeed upon life itself, with eyes unclouded by 'emotional distortion', with the eyes of the dead.

The questions of the oppressor's responsibility and ability to respond have always posed thorny problems in patriarchy, even for those sensitive to the plight of the oppressed. In *Animal Liberation*, Peter Singer maintains that 'it should not be assumed that the people named [as abusive to animals in research] are especially evil or cruel people. They are doing what they were trained to do, and what thousands of their colleagues do.'[27] The people named are not perceived as 'especially evil or cruel' people because in societies dominated by the 'ideology of cultural sadism', as Kathleen Barry has called it, violent acts are neutralised by virtue of being so common. In the case of animal experimentation, these violent acts are admired (published and replicated) and the actors honoured (tenured and funded).

Astonishing cruelty to animals can be legitimated in this way. As Roger Ulrich, who pioneered work on pain-elicited aggression in the rat, said: 'I ended up doing things to animals that really made me sick. But I rationalized it. I thought science could do anything, that it could solve our social problems.'[28] Ulrich stopped doing animal research on the grounds that it is 'a repugnant and socially irrelevant practice'. Unfortunately for animals, many 'thousands of [his] colleagues' have not followed suit.

When animal experimentation *is* criticised, students, teachers and researchers alike fall back on the two most common justifications:

(1) experimentation on live animals is necessary to human welfare; and (2) researchers follow strict guidelines that minimise animal suffering. What is human welfare? Better poisons, better chemicals, better cosmetics, better drugs, better behaviour, better brains, better genes? Acceptable levels of unacceptable carcinogenic materials that have invaded everyone's home? Fewer diseases? The dubious benefits of organ transplants? Making babies in petri dishes? Clones? Human hybrids? Genetically engineered life-forms? *Millions* of animals suffer and are sacrificed (killed) yearly for all this 'welfare'.[29]

Despite the impression given to the public that the major purpose of animal experimentation is to find cures for human diseases, only an infinitesimal part of animal research is directed to that end – and much of that could be done by using alternative methods.[30] For example, in his defence of animal experimentation, Gordon Hankinson, Director of the Foster Bio-Medical Research Laboratory at Brandeis University, only pointed to medical progress. He specifically named the polio vaccine as one of the 'many health problems' solved through animal research.[31] Yet in reality, the history of the polio vaccine is as follows: the Salk (1953) and Sabine (1956) vaccines are produced from viruses grown in *human* embryonic tissues. Animals, notably monkeys, were used in the initial research on polio by growing the virus in their nervous systems. This practice was abandoned for lack of results in 1949, when Enders found the alternative that worked better.[32]

Most animal experimenters are intellectually dishonest about the real goal of their research. As Richard Ryder, who coined the term 'speciesism' to denote human prejudice and discrimination in favour of the human species and against members of other species, pointed out, they 'are basically *conformers* who do not question what is expected of them . . . like most men they seek security and success and in order to achieve these ends they know that it pays to toe the line'.[33] So, if the truth be told, the real goal of scientific research is the *personal* 'welfare' of those involved.

As for 'guidelines', the very fact that they are needed indicates that researchers are unable to determine the limits of humane treatment and regulate themselves accordingly. Therefore, their professional organisations periodically issue a set of 'guidelines' aimed at limiting abuse of animals in housing, surgical and laboratory practices, adherence to which is basically on the 'honour system'. In all cases, the bottom line is the avoidance of 'unnecessary pain'. This is a relative expression and unfortunately it is relative to the 'needs' of the experimenters, not of the animals. As W. Lane-Petter expressed it in *Animals for Research*:

> To get maximum information out of [the experimental animal], by calibrating and using it to the best advantage, is sensible economy as well as profitable research. An understanding of the nature, capabilities, and limitations of the animal is also likely to lead to its humane use; an end *which may be incidental* but is always desirable.[34] (emphasis added)

This language clearly shows the emotional wasteland of the animal experimenter who combines scientific detachment with business interest, his concerns being efficiency and success. When one reaches the point at which one has to specify what humane treatment is, and name it *incidental*, one has lost all sense of kinship with other creatures.

Our common bond with animals is *natural* (of nature), *normal* (of the norm), and healthy (*whole*some). This is the way 'primitive' communities under goddess worship *experienced* all creatures' common bond to Mother Earth. In the age of Science and Technology, the scientists *experiment* upon this connection. They splice genes, dissect brains, manipulate behaviour to provide us with ways to 'promote human welfare' without slackening our commitment to fast-paced, necrophilic modern living.[35]

Ultimately, the desecrator of animal life ends up desecrating all life including his own, for he reduces life to discrete mechanisms of measurable quantity. He denies the complex interaction of all life systems, within and without the individual animal, plant, human being. He denies the political, social and economic elements that come into play in that interaction and inform self-perception, perception of others, emotions, motivation and reason. In the end, he has amassed 'crushing' amounts of information but has grown not at all in knowledge or understanding. For as Joan McIntyre, whose words always reflect a spirit deeply connected to Life, said when speaking of the whales slaughtered in the interest of Science:

> We can pile up the tables and weights and lengths and ages and measures until it reaches the sky, but it won't get us an understanding of the living

creature. The way to understand a living creature is to live respectfully in its presence, to approach it with tact, grace and love.[36]

Manufacturers of life: the animal breeders

'Progress' in the sciences and industry has created an exorbitant demand for laboratory animals. In the area of chemical substances alone, tests and more tests on animals are 'needed' to meet increasing government regulations before the 50,000 existing chemicals can continue to be used, and those 300-400 new ones manufactured every year can be deemed 'safe' and marketed for use. Toxicity testing of these and other man-made pollutants as well as medical, behavioural and genetic research take a tremendous toll of animal lives in laboratories. These lives are supplied largely through the services of breeding laboratories that can produce a complete assortment of test animals, including 'germ-free' ones.

Breeding is a clean word, a good word. It signifies the generating process, the bringing forth into the world of offspring by hatching or gestation. Breeding connotes ideas of nurture and protection, such as to 'brood' – the shelter a bird affords its young with its wings and body warmth. Metaphorically, to brood is to ponder, to meditate in gloom and gloom was originally nothing more than the colour yellow, like the August moon, like broom in bloom, and ripe golden fruit. It follows that a breeder is one that breeds and broods, one that mates, hatches, gestates, nurtures, and meditates.

Animal breeders could not be more undeserving of the name for their activities could not be more remote from mothering. The breeding of laboratory animals is a highly refined science which requires the collaboration of veterinarians, geneticists, neurologists and legions of other technicians who play the role that belongs by right to the female and heredity. Animal breeders have usurped the female role. Their attempts to 'improve' heredity is a corruption of animal integrity that fits into the pattern of objectification that permeates the culture.

The following examples will give an idea of the scale and economic magnitude of this enterprise. The Charles River Laboratory in North Wilmington, Massachusetts, whose founder and president was Henry Foster, is the largest systematic breeder of laboratory animals in the world. In 1979 it grossed $30 million by breeding rats, mice, hamsters, rabbits, guinea pigs and rhesus monkeys, the latter on two Caribbean islets off the Florida coast. It sells *18 million animals a year* to universities, government agencies, and manufacturing companies – Revlon, Dupont, General Foods, and hundreds of others, many of which are international companies. It operates in the United States, Europe and Japan. It is adding 'plants' in Canada and Great Britain.[37]

Hazelton Laboratories in Vienna, Virginia, sells a package that satisfies both the clients' and government's regulations. They supply the research, the equipment, and the animals – 'the razor blades of the business', as Hazelton's president, Kirby L. Cramer, calls the animals. The company styles itself a 'leading primate importer' and has bred 6,400 monkeys from 1975–80. It has increased the import and breeding programmes of primates and canines in order to meet new Food and Drug Administration product-testing requirements as well as the demands of genetic research. None the less, because of its close resemblance to human physiology, the rhesus monkey is in such high demand as a research animal that the waiting list is two to three years.

MOL Enterprises of Oregon vies with Charles River and Hazelton Laboratories to fill the growing demand for primates. MOL claims that it imports rhesus monkeys from Bangladesh. In one of its advertisements the customer is urged: 'Order Now! Country of origin export permits and documentation provided.'[38] Permits and documentation do not obscure the fact that these companies are trafficking in animals in ways that recall the slave and prostitute trades.[39] In all cases, living creatures are taken from their habitats and social units, separated from their kin, forcibly handled and transported to various destinations where they meet a sordid fate.

As I mentioned before, even the strictest guidelines for the 'care' of laboratory animals do not ensure that animals supplied to researchers will be treated 'humanely'. In 1978, Prime Minister Morarji Desai of India banned the export of rhesus monkeys to the United States citing violations of a previous agreement which specified that the animals would not be used in medical research except under humane conditions. At that time, Desai stated: 'There is no difference between cruelty to animals and cruelty to human beings.'[40] Taken at face value, Desai's statement and reaction appear to reflect an egalitarian attitude toward animals and humans as well as a sensitivity to the plight of animals used in research. However, the very fact of having authorised the exportation of monkeys for experimental purposes in the first place was in itself an act of cruelty. The banality of cruelty in patriarchal cultures ensures the proliferation of 'low-level' cruelty (as in low-level radiation, low-level carcinogens, 'humane' animal experimentation) and the continued toleration of these intolerable 'safe'/'moral' levels.

Women attuned to the many faces of misogyny can recognise not only the cruelty of the animal breeders' large-scale exploitation of life but the attitude of contempt/disgust for Nature – animal – woman that underlies it. Thus Foster conquered nature and improved upon her work by developing a 'specific pathogen-free' (SPF) rodent, an animal 'free' from the 'common diseases' transmitted to it at birth by its *'unclean* mother'.

> The procedure employed in producing gnotobiotes, or germ-free animals, is the aseptic removal of the fetuses from a gravid [pregnant] female by caesarean section, and their introduction and maintenance in a sterile environment . . . with a clean foster-mother – a lactating female from another SPF colony, or preferably from a gnotobiote colony having recently littered.[41]

In this and the following description of the methods used in the 'aseptic removal' of foetuses from a 'gravid' female, the emphasis is on procedure and technicians. All trace of life is erased except by inference, as if incidental to the procedure itself. Moreover, a profound disgust towards the female body functions emerges from under this polished gel of neutrality. A female is not pregnant, she is gravid. She is not hairless. She is depilated. Her womb is repugnant – infested with germs. Thus she is 'sacrificed' (killed) and the life within her is sterilised in plastic 'chambers'. The first method developed in 1946 by Reyniers

> involves elevating the gravid, depilated, sacrificed female to a taut plastic membrane in the base of a surgical isolator. A full 10-15 minutes is available after respiration stops in the sacrificed mother. The technician, with his arms in surgical gloves, performs a hysterectomy from within the sterile chamber lifting the intact gravid uterus through the surgical membrane in the floor of the plastic isolator into the chamber proper.[42]

The second method pioneered in 1959 by Foster consists of

performing an aseptic hysterectomy on a depilated gravid female killed by
cervical fracture [breaking her neck], then introducing the entire uterus
and contents into the surgical, sterile isolator *via* a germicidal liquid
trap.[43]

Pregnant rodents left to their own natural cycles are likely to
deliver their litters between 11 p.m. and 6 a.m. However, caesarian
surgery is 'awkward and tedious' *for the technician* at those hours.
Accordingly, 'progesterone injections daily from the 17th day [are
given, and] in a high percentage of cases, delay normal parturition so
that day time surgery can be undertaken, virtually eliminating all-
night vigils'.[44] Unable to bring forth life on his own, man simulates
the power of female generativity by manipulating her processes with
drugs, forcing her to yield in *his* time, and threatening and/or taking
her very life. In *The Hidden Malpractice*, Gena Corea has analysed
the male take-over of the female reproductive processes. She noted
the following: 'Induction of labor is practiced for the doctor's convenience in spite of dangers to mother and child. . . . Provoking labor
allows doctors to plan schedules efficiently.'[45] Likewise, the
American mother is no longer 'an active child-bearer. . . . Now,
strapped and drugged, she is the object on which the doctor works and
her unborn baby is "the intrauterine patient".'[46] The only difference
between pregnant women and those gravid female rodents is that the
rodent is automatically sacrificed/killed.

Man is transforming nature, animals and women beyond recognition and making conceptual provisions for a smooth transition. As
Foster stated: 'Opinion is on the increase, as each month and year
passes, that the clean SPF animal is more truly representative of a
normal animal than its predecessor, the conventional animal' (emphasis added).[47] The manufactured, manipulated, 'living' product is
becoming the norm, first in the sense of being valued because it
serves man's purposes better and is more manageable than the 'conventional' variety, and eventually it will be the norm by virtue of being the only kind of animal around.

Animal breeders market this 'norm' in journals of the trade like so
many pieces of furniture. King Animals Laboratories, Inc. (Wisconsin) provides a repulsive example: 'The WORD is out! King is really
good. . . . You can trust King. . . . Compare their prices, their quality! Call collect, compare. . . . We guarantee you will be completely

satisfied.' In a typical issue of *Laboratory Animal Science* (February 1979, 29 (1)), no fewer than seventeen breeding companies offered animals for sale with equally shocking sales pitches. Their 'products' are frequently drawn in poses and costumes that conform to gender stereotypes: subordinate female animals lure, allure, and invite abuse. Dominant male animals command. The captions speak volumes. Harlan Industries, Inc., of Indiana declaims: 'We're the Harlan bunch. You should get to know the Harlan bunch. . . . [Harlan rodents are] Brought Up To Serve You Better.' Engle Laboratory Animals, Inc., also of Indiana, displays a long-lashed, pregnant hamster with the caption: 'Real anxious to please you.' These advertisements clearly address a male clientele titillated by images of coy, 'attractive' females smiling all the way to the sacrifice.

Other companies advertising in the pages of these journals specialise in providing the accoutrements of animal experimentation – testing equipment, 'home cages', bedding, food, watering systems, drugs and accessories such as lab coats for *Es*, and for *Ss*, the 'completely washable' guillotine that will decapitate 'instantly' not only rats and mice but 'other lab animals' as well. Lab-Caging Systems offers a complete line of aluminium wares. Pictures of these metal 'home cages' must be seen to be believed. The only 'animals' they are about to house are mini-skirted, white-coated *women* draped over the cages, stroking the metal in seeming eagerness to enter the larger ones themselves.

For the *billions* of animals whose fate it has been and will be to be bred by men for experimental purposes, this is all a nightmare. For those involved on all levels of the trade in animals, the pay-off is blood money.

Consumers of life: the public

> You don't need to be a hen to know a bad egg.
>
> Proverb

To give this discussion a realistic focus, I want to make it clear that I use the word *consumer* in the context of consumerism, not in the natural sense of consuming in order to stay alive. Consumerism is a way of life based on the consumption of goods for purposes of feeding artificially created desires. To distinguish essential need from artificial desire or, for that matter, trying to define need can lead to a tangle of arguments that would take me too far afield. I assume that the intelligent reader knows the difference and knows that we consume beyond the point of satisfying essential needs.

The manufacture of new products goes hand in hand with the promotion of media images that shape people's 'needs' and ideas of 'the good life' in order to encourage consumption. These processed/synthetic items intended for human consumption/use are tested for 'safety' on animals. Consequently, the consumers who buy both the image and the product also contribute directly to the degradation and artificiality of life as well as to animal pain.

Safety evaluation procedures for drugs, cosmetics, toiletries, household products, food additives, plastics, etc. consist of such things as the 'writhing' and the 'LD/50' tests. These tests produce intense suffering in animals. The 'writhing test' is so named because of the agonised way the animals react to irritants injected in their abdomens. The 'LD (lethal dose)/50 test' consists 'of force-feeding a group of animals a specific substance until half of them die'.[48]

Peter Singer has documented the LD/50 test performed at the Mead Johnson Research Center at Evansville, Indiana, and at the Huntingdon Research Centre, Huntingdon, England. The animals used were rabbits, rhesus monkeys, squirrel monkeys, cats, rats, dogs and mice. In one of the tests, Amidephrine Mesylate, a nasal decongestant 'was administered to the animals by mouth, by injection, into the nostrils, and tested for irritancy on the eyes and penises of rabbits. . . . The LD/50 values were determined for all species.'[49]

Animals are the targets of research and women are the targets of marketing. From dietetic foods and beverages to make-up that claims to give a 'natural look', to sprays and cleansers that deodorise and sterilise the home, women are persuaded to accept a thoroughly denaturalised environment and appearance. For instance, the latest advance in the cosmetic industry is a 3 million dollar utilisation of NASA's computer technology. Women can now choose from a number of 'high-tech faces' painted for them by 'make-up artists' (men) and displayed on a special video monitor. If the 'artist' 'feels the woman needs a wider mouth or thinner lips, he can show her how to do this without removing [her] own lipstick. He can also teach her the newest techniques in applying make-up.'[50]

In another development, the computerised skin analyser, the 'beauty adviser' 'uses a wand stroked over the woman's face to activate a lipid meter, a hydrometer and a skin-color analyzer' and then gives make-up recommendations.[51] The technology is a spin-off from the male war machine, the hucksters are 'women' executives, the intended victims of these latest illusion-making machines (the 'new image') are the women already destroyed by the myth of youth and beauty, and the underlying victims are the animals on whom the products have been tested.

Food is a basic requirement, but processed food, the contents of which have been manipulated to the point of requiring toxicity testing, provides another instance of an artificial need. These foods may calm hunger, save time and work, provide a semblance of social contact while they are being consumed, etc., but they do not nourish. What they satisfy is the desire for convenience (even if that convenience is deleterious to life) and the desire to conform to the physical, social, and mental standards dictated by the culture. For example, the physical model for women in the 1980s was the 'skinny girl' look, i.e. anorexic. Even so, 60 per cent of Americans are overweight. Accordingly, special diets and beverages tested on animals are 'needed'. These diets are not nourishing and create other health problems for which additional animal testing is then also 'needed'.

It is sometimes argued that education to the horrors of the animal research underlying consumerism would heighten people's sensibility by bringing them back to their senses and that the 'educated consumer' would boycott the products for which these tests are used. Assuming consumers then cared enough, what price would they pay in order to spare animal pain? In an over populated, urbanised world, it is easier to depend on the foods offered in supermarkets than to boycott those foods and look for alternatives. And in general, consumers are encouraged to depend on looks and material goods to satisfy a morbid craving for approval and a false sense of self-esteem. Being insatiable by their very nature, these cravings 'necessitate' further consumerism.

Consumerism thrives on the apathy and thoughtlessness of the consumer.[52] Thus, people carry shopping bags stamped with the slogan 'Educated Consumer' but do not carry placards protesting the torture of the animals used to market the items that fill those bags. The slogan may be 'clever' but it means nothing except 'education' to more consumerism. As a group consumers expend considerable time, energy and money on evaluating advertisements, comparing products, deciding what to buy – thus indirectly supporting the industries that bring them 'new', superfluous products. On the other hand, as a group consumers expend virtually nothing to educate themselves about the animal research by which those industries operate. A sense of powerlessness also underlies and encourages consumerism. Even though consumers spend more and more on the 'good things in life', a *good life* seems ever elusive and unattainable. Consumers ultimately attempt to deny that feeling of powerlessness by acquiring and/or consuming more 'new and improved', 'state of the art' 'goods'.

Education to the horrors of animal research may sensitise some people enough to influence their life-styles. But for those in the majority who have never left the city other than on mediated outings and therefore lack the appreciation that comes from real experience with the ways of nature,[53] changing their 'convenience' and store-bought self-images in order to minimise the plight of laboratory animals is not likely to occur. In particular, us cities, where the trend to consumerism originated and is most invasive, are the very symbol of all that is antithetical to nature. They are acres of concrete and glass, swarming with people who work in man-made environments in order to procure for themselves the commodities they consume at a prodigious rate. Natural reminders are scarce: a few trees,[54] a few birds, a few rodents.

For consumer education about the sadistic treatment of research animals to be effective, it must be accompanied by a thorough revolution in our entire value system. We live in a self-centred, self-indulgent culture. To break away from it requires an act of will: the will to replace experiment with genuine experience of the wider world, the will to give our consciousness the breathing space it needs in order to distinguish the programmed from the real. It requires going beyond people-centredness and the exclusive representation of the human point of view, a sharpening of the mind so that our choices may be wise and our assessment of 'news' judicious. It requires patience, the shedding of prejudice, the willingness to change many of our habits and thought patterns. In short, it requires learning to love life.

The rationalisations of animal experimentation

> But for those not yet touched by the disease and
> certainly for the generations as yet unborn,
> prevention is the imperative need.
>
> Rachel Carson, *Silent Spring*

> An ounce of prevention is worth a pound of
> cure
>
> Proverb

Physical health

Much of animal research is said to be conducted to gain a better understanding of human diseases in order 'to save lives' and promote health. As the American Cancer Society has stated: 'Important medical discoveries have been made, or confirmed, by such experiments (on animals), saving countless human lives.'[55] This reasoning rationalises the assault upon the integrity of nature manifested in all animal experimentation. It is typical of patriarchal control strategy whereby the integrity of matter (living and non-living) is broken, artificially restored/reconstituted, and marketed in such a way (cure, improvement, etc.) as to elicit gratitude. Mary Daly has named this syndrome 'sado-sublimation' and has shown that, although it is designed to incapacitate all life, it is particularly devastating to women. It manipulates women into worshipping their disguised tormentors, thus sinking them deeper into helplessness and dependency.[56]

Seeking to solve health problems is real in so far as the proliferation of diseases is real. However it must be kept in mind that this proliferation is a function of man's deadly interferences with life processes and the wholesomeness of 'the environment'. If health were a genuine concern, scientists would turn their minds to restoring healthy conditions for all life. By fixating on disease, they draw attention away from the patriarchal mania to control, which derives from the fear of being subject to nature. This biophobia underlies all animal research, no matter what the rationalisation.

Etymologically and experientially, to be healthy is to be sound of mind and body. It is to be intact – not broken, damaged or injured. It is to be complete – containing all of one's elements or parts. It is to be whole – not divided against oneself. Health is the natural state of any creature able to take what it needs from a wholesome, supportive environment and utilise it for its wellbeing. In this natural state, the synchrony between the needs of an organism and the environment's sustaining capacities allows for a mutual reciprocity whereby all organisms 'know' how to maintain their integrity.

In the natural state, health is the norm and disease is abnormal. The organism breaks down either because it cannot find what it needs in its environment and/or only finds what is deleterious to its wellbeing. It might also be attacked by stronger, hostile elements in the environment which it is unable to overcome. The state of disease is an *unnatural* state wherein the delicate, sustaining balance between an organism and its ecology is undone. Comparatively few organisms are diseased beyond their natural capacity to heal themselves. Given a disproportionate increase in the numbers of diseased organisms, life on earth would collapse.

A glaring reversal occurs in the cultural state. Disease has become so commonplace that health can be characterised as the absence of specific disease rather than the state of integrity, of being whole/ sound. In addition, disease is an expectation reflected in the emphasis on regular check-ups for 'early detection signals', mandatory health insurance programmes, the increasing number of 'societies' and organisations dedicated to milking private and public funds to support *more* animal experimentation and thereby conquer disease, and in the widespread publicity of the details of horrible diseases, newest technologies and breakthroughs. These, together with 'heart-rending' stories of innocent children, overburdened mothers, and hard-working fathers about to die for lack of a 'cure' have made a nation of hypochondriacs desperate to name their deep-seated malaise and buy the remedy.

The proliferation of exercise programmes, 'health' clubs, 'health' foods, dietary supplements, over-the-counter as well as prescribed drugs, personal therapies and/or personal libraries bulging with the works of pop psychologists and physicians, all of this speaks loud and clear of a widespread unwholesomeness of body and mind and of the huge profits to be had in catering to the unhealthy. There is but a short step from disease as the norm to disease renamed as 'health'. A Boston-based chain of 'health' clinics claims to be 'yours in sickness and in health', and has exchanged the word 'doctor' for that of 'provider'. Thus, one's provider affords the grateful 'patient' a commodity the 'patient' unknowingly has (health). Insidiously, the medical establishment has undermined people's self-knowledge and created a state of dependency that ensures the 'need' for more providers, medical technology and animal research.

Despite all the rhetoric concerning health, there has been an increase in cancer, coronary heart disease, and birth defects. In addition, new diseases have developed (AIDS, toxic shock syndrome) and the number of 'maladjusted' people has soared. Since most of these disorders spring from the conditions of life under patriarchal rule, animal research cannot lead to their cure. Cancer and depression are two cases in point. Both are increasingly common disorders with acknowledged origins in environmental/social conditions. Both have already taken large tolls of animal lives in research and continue to do so. Yet far from having been eliminated, they have reached epidemic proportions.

Obviously, it is not because scientists have yet to find the cure for cancer that cancer proliferates. Rather, cancer proliferates because so very little is done to reduce the burden of stress and poisons which man imposes upon life systems. Scientists are said to have made 'great progress' in understanding cancer by reducing it to genetic factors. They hope 'to devise ways to block it [the genetic events (*sic*) that cause cells to grow out of control], thus preventing the development of cancer or curing it once it is detected'.[57] This biological, cellular intervention completely begs the question of the environmental sources of cancer. Inducing disease in animals is an unhealthy act both for the agent (the experimenter) and the victim. By definition, un-health cannot bring about health.

Isolating any part of the organism as if it were a thing in itself independent of the whole is the mechanistic approach to disease/health that pervades science. The organism is trivialised, as in the statement that it is 'no great trick' to invade our genes.[58] Its body is infected with disease which is cast as a wily and dangerous enemy, the better to display the researcher's genius. Thus, J. Michael Bishop, professor of microbiology at the University of California and recipient of the Lasker Award for his contribution to 'our' understanding of cancer, commented on the latest breakthrough in cancer research (identifying the malfunction of the oncogene): 'After centuries of bewilderment, the human [*sic*] intellect has finally laid hold of cancer with a grip that may eventually extract the deadly secrets of the disease'.[59]

Another 'new cancer clue' has been isolated from the blood of mice by researchers at the Memorial Sloan-Kettering Cancer Center in New York. This substance eliminates cancers in other mice. The evidence 'supports the concept that normal animals have a biochemical surveillance system which enables them to fight off cancer repeatedly during the course of their lives'.[60] All of these animals could have been spared if researchers in particular and people in general set any store by common sense, for these results show that in a natural state, health is the norm. The real question to address with respect to cancer is whether the oncogenes or any other part of an organism malfunction when they are *not* being asked to react to massive and unnatural amounts of carcinogenic pollutants. But this question will not seriously be entertained, as it is more profitable to continue cancer research and violate more lives – animals, plants, and humans – than to eliminate the major carcinogenic materials that pour out from the vast industrial complex considered *vital* to a *healthy* economy.

Concern for health is a lie made even more patently clear when one looks at the food industry. It participates in cancer research through testing carcinogenic additives and pesticide and herbicide residues. It contributes to cancer by marketing carcinogens. Thus, it has reversed the function of food from health-giving to disease-inducing, all the while seducing the public with images of health and strength. The US Environmental Protection Agency (EPA) in charge of monitoring safety standards works hand in hand with the animal research establishment and the manufacturers of poisons. According to Jim Davis of the EPA's Pesticides and Toxic Substance Division, 'Often the carcinogens we find [in food] are considered very low risk.[61] Society as a whole has to make some sort of determination about what level of risk is acceptable'.[62] What is 'society' to do after considering the following: there are 900 registered pesticides used in foodstuffs and believed to cause cancer. Poison-coated fruit and vegetables are not subject to the Delaney Clause that 'protects' processed foods.[63] As agricultural production is becoming more centralised (sprayed and treated en masse), the choice of products becomes less possible, particularly in large urban areas. At best, consideration of these facts leads to great perplexity.

Thus as health, which is ours by right, eludes and recedes, researchers in their frenzy draw in more and more animals to test the *risk* levels of disease – which they call 'health'. As for those individuals able to help themselves, Joan Gussow, head of the nutrition programme at Columbia University Teachers College in New York, has stated:

> If you don't eat anything your Neolithic ancestors wouldn't have recognized, you'll probably be all right. It's not difficult to choose a healthy diet from whole foods. In fact, it's almost impossible not to. But it is extremely difficult to choose a healthy diet from eighteen thousand items of processed foods.[64]

She went on to recommend:

> Go visit the farmer. Buy foods that come from close to home – the closer the better. Buy simple foods, with relatively little processing, foods that are whole (i.e. healthy) and fresh. Part of what people have to do is *think*.[65]

Thinking means in part assessing the cost to life – animal, human, planetary – of technological claims to health. Feminists are in a vanguard position for we are eminently prepared to detect patriarchal manipulative tactics wherever they are manifested. Processing is a technique we have already analysed with respect to women in patriarchy. Women have been processed in the same way as foods: breaking down, removal of essential parts, replacement with man-made additives, reconstruction into artificial aggregates. In addition, we know from experience that any argument in support of oppression is a lie, no matter how disguised. In the case that concerns me here, experimental animals are the oppressed. But it is obvious that their oppression is also ours, and that the pain they are made to endure for our 'health' backfires onto us as disease.

Crucial questions, such as why we allow and continue to support the production of acknowledged causes of disease – nuclear radioactivity, poison gas, chemical warfare, germ warfare, industrial and agricultural pollutants, alcohol, tobacco, processed foods, and so on – are not taken seriously. They are obscured by the stardust of 'progress', 'gross national product', 'national security', 'personal freedom', which translate into jobs, high living standards, and fat money for those in command. Connecting disease with the way we choose to live requires that we recognise how as individuals and as a society we daily renew our commitment to disease. We need to be aware of the *whole* problem and be prepared for radical rather than piecemeal change.

Mental health

Turning to the area of 'mental health', we see that animal research is used once more to rationalise the status quo and that, as in the case of physical health, the 'cures' for mental disorders found and/or tested on animals further undermine rather than promote health (wholesomeness). Since these 'cures' at best provide temporary relief through electric shock, drugs, or an hour of allowable (i.e. under the therapist's control) real emotion such as grief or anger, they are ineffective in the long run because illusory and unrelated to the source of the dis-ease. Like most physical diseases, 'neuroses' are largely the result of unwholesome social conditions.

A case in point is depression. Depression is a manipulated state, a counterfeit emotion characterised by extreme passivity (dulled senses, inactivity, lack of interest in one's surroundings). It is, in fact, a chilled, bloodless, lifeless state of physical and emotional helplessness resulting from human power games. In their experimental investigation of the aetiology of this state, Bruce Overmier and Martin Seligman forced eighty-eight 'mongrel dogs' into a powerless situation by exposing them to strong electric shocks to their footpads while preventing them from escaping. The experimenters administered as many as 640 shocks to some of the dogs – at a rate of one shock on the average of every nine seconds. Predictably the dogs 'learned helplessness' – i.e. they did not attempt to escape from shock when subsequently given an opportunity to do so.[66] Rather, broken in spirit, will and emotion, they helplessly and hopelessly submitted to the painful stimuli the experimenters foisted upon them. If an individual, not working on an 'approved' project, were to take his dog and out of curiosity subject the animal to a fraction of these manipulations, that individual would probably be reported to the 'authorities' (animal welfare societies), and the animal would be taken from him. To actually make a career of it would qualify that person as a candidate for rehabilitation in a mental hospital.

Other luminaries of psychological research have abused animals in the name of depression, presumably so as to bring about its cure. Harry Harlow at the Primate Research Center, Madison, Wisconsin, put young monkeys in separate stainless steel pits, leaving them there for up to forty-five days. Predictably, the monkeys stared at the walls, looking up to the shaft of light above, immobile, depressed.[67]

One cure for depression is sought in 'therapeutic' drugs which alter the chemistry of the body and/or brain. Researchers in this area find it very 'exciting' that they can counteract the effects of stress-induced helplessness with their potions. To Jay Weiss and his associates

the behavioral phenomenon seen in dogs [helplessness] is even *more exciting* when its physiological basis [decreased activity of norepinephrine in the brain] is acknowledged and understood . . . Environment, brain and behavior are thereby brought together.[68] (emphasis added)

Environment, brain and behaviour might be brought together in some perverted fashion, but the animals in this research are torn asunder. Drugs 'protect' the rats against the after effects of severe stressors such as forced swims in cold water (2°C) and severe inescapable shocks. This protection means that the animal can sustain these traumas without showing subsequent behavioural deficits, their depression and helplessness being temporarily allayed by the introduction of chemicals in their brains.

Clearly, the animals need to be protected not from the natural reactions of their brains but from the human beings who force them to endure abusive, stressful conditions, who find helplessness 'exciting', and whose so-called cures consist of further violations of animal integrity. Such fragmentation (fracturing of the self) weakens individual power to grasp the true nature of 'the problem' and thus to act upon it independently and intelligently. Women are especially susceptible to this dis-ease. We have been drawn into the energy-draining patriarchal sado-sublimation syndrome and handed over to 'therapies' that reinforce depression by further obscuring the real source of our helplessness and that punish our anger, which is the very thing that would energise and save us from it.

Another means offered to control 'undesirable' emotional states is direct intervention into brain sites (*sic*) responsible for them. Thus Dr José Delgado, professor of physiology at Yale University School of Medicine suggests that

[the] basic mechanism [of very difficult therapeutic problems] might be traced to the increased reactivity of specific areas of the brain. All these disturbances could be cured, or at least diminished, if we had a better knowledge of their anatomical and functional bases and could inhibit the activity of neurons responsible for the phenomena.[69]

The following experiment by Delgado represents one of his attempts to gain this knowledge by raping the brain/mind of animals. He first transformed a chimpanzee (Paddy) into a cyborg.* With 100 intra-cerebral electrodes implanted in his skull, Paddy was then made to 'interface' with a computer which, upon recognising certain wave patterns, activated Paddy's 'stimulator' in another area of his brain. Delgado controlled this experiment until Paddy's brain wave pattern in that area was reduced to only 1 per cent of normal occurrence. By then, Paddy's spirit, as well, was completely broken.

> As the spindles disappear, Paddy becomes strangely quiet. Though he was a lively chimp before that experiment, now he just sits in his chair, performing whatever tasks are required of him, and barely moving. He doesn't look at the food pellets that are given him as rewards; nor, in most cases, does he eat them. He doesn't dare be aroused by anything. For weeks after the end of this experiment, Paddy remains as humble as a whipped dog.[70]

It is not to be imagined that such 'therapeutic' experiences are limited to laboratory animals. Dr Robert Heath of Tulane University has been stimulating (and destroying) areas in the brains of humans for decades. Using theory and observations he derived from his brain experiments with cats, in 1950 he implanted an electrode in the septal area of a schizophrenic patient with the stated intention of 'bringing the individual out of the sleep-like state of reverie and helping him to make a better interpretation of reality'.[71] When he stimulated the brain of another patient who had just attempted to commit suicide by jumping from the roof, the man started to smile and said he 'felt good'.[72]

Deprived of true emotions arising from their own experiences, both animal subjects and human patients controlled by brain stimulation

---

* The word itself combines two roots – Greek *kybernan*, to steer, and *organism*. It is defined in *Merriam-Webster* as 'a human being who is linked to one or more mechanical devices upon which his vital physiological functions depend'.

are made tractable and responsive to the desires of the doctor/therapist. Such a state is characteristic of many women. They pass from one depressive episode to another, temporarily eased by drugs, therapy, alcohol, junk food, television, and periodic injections of male approval. When women recognise the true nature of our violation, our reaction is not depression but creative grief or rage, as the case warrants. In this culture, these genuine emotions are hard to come by as grief is allowed only to the extent that it does not interfere with a woman's responsibilities. As for just rage, it is perceived and treated as anti-social, destructive behaviour, especially reprehensible in women.

The work of Samuel Corson of the Ohio State University with dogs provides another model for emotional flattening through the use of drugs to induce adjustment to the intolerable.

> Within a period of one hour [amphetamine] dramatically transformed the incorrigible, vicious, antisocial warrior [the dog, Jackson] into a peaceful, cooperative lovable dog who not only permitted himself to be petted but appeared to enjoy the social amenities, as evidenced by his general appearance and by the kind of whimpering one sees in properly reared pets.[73]

'Properly reared pets' have a great deal in common with the well-adjusted women and people of colour whom the white man has conquered/colonised/enslaved. The dog is considered to be 'properly reared' when it whimpers and allows itself to be petted. Women are well bred, well adjusted when they efface themselves behind joyless smiles, limp voices and demure mannerisms that make them tractable. Slaves and colonised people are well adjusted when they assimilate white values and behaviour patterns and allow themselves to be petted, i.e. show deference to whites. The master achieves and maintains his dominance by means of a brutal training that punishes health ('incorrigible, vicious, antisocial')* and rewards conformity and submission ('peaceful, cooperative, lovable') in those dominated.

In the scientists' struggles to conquer physical and mental diseases, animal research is chosen precisely because it affords the researcher

---

* Jackson's 'viciousness' was a healthy, wholesome resistance to man-handling – strapping in the Pavlovian harness.

unconditional control over 'mindless nature'. We have seen this work referred to as 'exciting'. It certainly is profitable. We have also seen that the rationalisations focus first on bringing health to society and second, on minimising risks to human patients by research on animals. Sickness of mind and body is endemic to patriarchy and no amount of animal research can remedy this. *Wholeness* is health. *Wholeness* is healing power. Being right with ourselves, we are right with the Earth, her creatures, and her elements. Approached with respect, the Earth will then be able to draw on her energy and heal herself. In *Daughters of Copper Woman*, Anne Cameron speaks of women creating our wholeness again which, to my mind, will become manifest throughout the universe as health.

> Women are bringing the pieces of the truth together. Women are believing again that we have a right to be whole. Scattered pieces from the black sisters, from the yellow sisters, from the white sisters, are coming together, trying to form a whole, and it can't form without the pieces we [Native American women] have saved and cherished.[74]

Happiness

How dare you sport thus with life?

Mary Shelley, *Frankenstein*

Scientists seeking to discover 'the mystery of life' in the genes and in the chemistry of the body, as well as in 'the secrets of the brain' and the principles of behaviour, point to 'happiness' as their ultimate goal. In their scientific quest for happiness they make it a quantifiable category of knowledge having little to do with the actual *experience* of happiness, and everything to do with achieving complete independence from nature and women. The man freed from these unfortunate impediments is the happy man. José Delgado has described the challenge as follows:

> A decisive step in the evolution of man and in the establishment of his superiority over other living creatures was his gradual achievement of *ecological liberation*. Why should man accept unnecessary hardships. . . . Thus began the process of *man's ecological domination*, the victory of human intelligence over the fate of mindless nature.[75] (emphasis added)

Delgado's 'mindless nature' is what Freud had chosen to call Fate before the era of scientific breakthroughs in genetic and brain research. According to him, human 'independence of Fate' was the requisite for happiness, for it would better equip man to handle 'the pleasure principle' that was at the root of so much conflict and so many neuroses.

Even in the context of ultimate control, it is not immediately apparent that the female presence in the familiar word *happiness* is lost. Therefore, I want to look for a moment at the etymology of 'happiness' and related words and show how their meanings have been drastically reduced in the researcher's language of rationalisation. Moreover, although it is doubtful that anyone could find happiness in the researcher's idea of happiness, women in particular are certain never to find it there since we are not present in it.

'Happiness' comes from *happ*, a Nordic word for the good luck brought upon someone. This meaning survives in the word 'happen', as in 'Guess what happened to me today', or 'I wonder what will happen tomorrow.' Luck is by definition unpredictable. Tradition has always associated it with woman, as in the expression, Lady Luck. The Latin-based 'fortune' also means the luck that befalls one at the discretion of the female power, Fortuna. Luck *befalls* one, and so does chance (from Latin *cadere*, to fall), because both luck and chance are perceived to strike from unseen, unknown regions 'above' the earth, bringing something unusual and good.

'Felicity' is synonymous with happiness. Its Latin root and etymological connections with 'feminine' show even more clearly its association with female power. *Frui* (to enjoy) and *felic-* (fruitful) suggest rituals of fertility centred around nature and woman, whose regeneration always involves incalculable elements but whose fruitfulness is vital to the wellbeing of a community. The concepts of fate and destiny are also linked to happiness, luck, felicity, and chance. The Fates are traditionally represented as women dispensing to human lives whatever was decreed beforehand and constitutes human destiny. Their oracles were women sensitive to natural events. They used these events as omens, portents, auguries of happiness, that is, of the luck about to accrue on someone – or of the doom of impending misfortune.

It is clear from this brief excursion into etymology that happiness is intimately related to female power and that it is both unpredictable and uncontrollable. By contrast, the stated goals of science are prediction and control through direct manipulation. The claim that animal research brings happiness to human beings is thus a contradiction in terms. In their attempts to eliminate the unpredictable, researchers force the 'happ' out of happiness. The female element of spontaneity is likewise forced out in the process. Experimentation is the core of this forcing. There is nothing to happiness even before the experiment begins since its motivation is control. When the experiment is finished, there are 'results' computed from a mass of data and, for those who care to acknowledge it, a tremendous amount of animal pain. Happiness clearly cannot flow from these goals and procedures, either for the animals under experimentation or for the human beings for whose sakes this research is said to be undertaken.

Yet it is 'happiness' which is sought by those who chart and stimulate the brain, splice and recombine genes, manipulate environments so as to modify behaviour, hybridise the species and attempt to couple man with machine. These researchers would degut the species, as it were, emptying it of all that makes people human. They would restructure it into a new product that conforms to their vision of a happy world. Thus, their happiness is the absence of pain, absence of stress, absence of anxiety, absence of violence, disease, depression, pessimism, and so on. Above all, it is the absence of consciousness and the ethical functions of consciousness.

In this sense, happiness is the absence of right and wrong, the absence of choice. The 'new man' would be 'mindlessly happy' without possessing the awareness that he was being thoroughly manipulated into an illusion of happiness. He would be literally out of his mind without experiencing paranoia (paranoia: out of one's mind). In fact, he would not *experience* anything. He would merely receive sensations of varying intensities by mechanically activating his 'pleasure centers' programmed by the new technological elite. Such a 'man' is no better than an experimental object. Such a 'man' is no longer human.

There is ample documentation of the extent to which 'the technologists of control' are engaged in the redefining (re-shaping) of the human species in totalitarian and mechanistic terms.[76] For example, José Delgado believes that complete control of the brain will result in a 'psychocivilisation' through electrical stimulation of the brain (ESB) and produce a man 'happier, less destructive, and better balanced than present man'.[77] Robert Sinsheimer, president of the American

Biophysical Society, who experiments in coupling man and machine (bio-cybernetics), envisages a world peopled with geniuses and hopes that 'we [will] rid ourselves, along the way of "emotional anachronisms" like excess aggressiveness and pessimism'.[78]

Women do not need man's research in colonising the brain in order to know happiness. If asked the questions: What can you do to bring about a happier world? What can you do to make yourself happy? – a woman's answer would never be: I must control my violence and the violence of other women. A woman seeking happiness would most likely want to spin into a new awareness of her Self and find freedom and happiness *in her Self*.[79] Clearly, animal research aimed at restructuring the human species in man's image contributes nothing to women's quest for happiness.

Women do not as a whole think of happiness as a constant state but as a fluid quality of life welling up from the Self and expressed in relatedness to another. The notions of 'power over' and 'absence of . . .' are not present except as they relate to self-control and the freeing of the Self from dependency.

Charlotte Brontë	[Happiness comes from experiencing] firmer trust in myself and in my powers. *(Jane Eyre)*
Margaret Atwood	This above all, to refuse to be a victim. Unless I can do that I can do nothing. *(Surfacing)*
Kate Chopin	[From the only happy character in the book, a woman self-fulfilled in her art and in herself. Asked what it takes, she replies:] The courageous soul . . . The brave soul, the soul that dares and defies. *(The Awakening)*
George Eliot	The change was a very happy one to me, for the first sight of the Alps, with the setting sun on them . . . seemed to me like an entrance into heaven; and the three years of my life there were spent in a perpetual sense of exultation, as if from a draught of delicious wine, at the presence of Nature in all her awful loveliness. *(The Lifted Veil)*

Woman's happiness does not mean that she cannot be angry, and that she does not manifest that anger in aggression. But anger is a genuine feeling – men do not violate from anger, they violate from the will to dominate and from wanting to conform to the image of maleness. Jules H. Masserman, a psychoanalyst and neurologist at Northwestern University Medical School has unwittingly defined the essence of male aggression as 'an urgent assertion of omnipotence, invulnerability and immortality that leads man to seek absolute control over his material universe and deny death itself'.[80] Woman's aggression flows from protectiveness: a mother defending her child, a woman defending her Self. Anger does not need to be rationalised. Domination and male violence always do.

Without spontaneous experience there can be no happiness and there can be no spontaneous experience without our ability to collect and re-collect our sensations, feelings and images. Women know much about false memories. Being deprived of our gynocentric past, we have been led to believe that man's memories (history) constitute human reality. As Mary Daly pointed out, 'the fathers have recognized Memory as their enemy, and they have worked to destroy its vestiges in women'.[81] We have been led to dream man's dream of happiness. We have just recently come to re-collect the memories of *our* past and from this material we have begun to spin our dreams and draw the strength we need for our present happiness. From our past we learn to reconnect to nature, plants, animals, the earth, the sea, and to treat all with gentleness and care.

Now, from man's research we learn that our very memories can be jogged, formed, and erased through chemicals. Bernard Agranoff of Michigan University's Mental Health Research Institute has interfered with 'the machinery of the cell', blocking protein synthesis with drugs in animals in order to affect their newly-formed memories. In his words: 'With this much knowledge of protein synthesis, man [*sic*] can begin to think of examining the process of interfering with it in selective ways'.[82] Interfering with memories in any way is dangerous to one's integrity.[83] Doing it with scientific precision has devastating implications for women: without memories there are no dreams, no imagination, no future, and above all, no present. As Kady, craftswoman, put it, the memory of our history 'helps me dare to imagine that we might somehow break free'.[84] And what is happiness, in its original sense of sudden good fortune associated with female power, without our freedom?

Longevity

> I *cannot* live without my life! I *cannot* live without my soul!
>
> Emily Brontë, *Wuthering Heights*

Like the quests for health and happiness, the quest for longevity belongs to the patriarchal order of rifts and splittings. Man's violent separation from Mother Earth created a host of dichotomies demanding the invention of ideological systems whereby he could identify his place in the universe and rationalise the void behind his existence. No longer able to believe that in dying he would flow back to the stream of life ever-present in the Goddess he had murdered, he faced death alone in fear, guilt, and envy of Mother Earth's endless/ageless renewals. The quest for longevity has its origin here.

Longevity and its related concept, immortality, grow out of an awareness of time. Prehistoric burial sites contain evidence that the dead were provided with tribal cult objects, food and drink for their journey toward rebirth. This cyclical, regenerative perception of time–space and life–death is characteristic of all earth-worshipping societies, modified versions of which persisted well into patriarchal times. In this perspective of time and nature, longevity is an affirmation of life. It is the experience of being long-lived. As for immortality, it is a given in the ceaseless ebb and flow of Mother Earth.

By contrast, the *quest* for longevity and immortality emerges from a perception of time as linear and is grounded in the rejection of the body and its connection with Nature/Mother Earth. It reveals a morbid fear of ageing, an aversion to decay, and the denial of death. Longevity becomes a quantifiable commodity (an accumulation of years without regard to the quality of living), and immortality a static, boring state (an immutable condition devoid of the ancient notions of perpetual renewal epitomised by the regenerating cycles of Mother Earth). Longevity makes genealogy: so many sons to perpetuate the father's name. It makes history: a man's old age is an accomplishment (Methuselah). It makes politics: family, church, city, state and country governments are headed by dotty or tyrannical old men. It makes economics: old age is big business.

As a male value anchored in sex and power, longevity is a fixation on age and virility rather than a state of being long-lived, which implies continual growth in a healthy environment. That environment is lacking in societies that segregate the old in 'nursing' centres/homes, retirement villages, senior citizen housing . . . and that have spawned new sciences (geriatrics, gerontology) to 'deal with' the elderly. Growth is automatically stunted in these ghettoised and dependent conditions. The very expression 'senior citizen' referring to an old woman or an old man is an attempt to deny the process of ageing and decay and to ward off thoughts of one's impending death. As an expression, it serves to keep an old woman split from the Crone in her and deprives her of a public naming and an awareness of her long life that might catapult her back into the cycle of life.

The quest for longevity is a non-quest requiring constant activity (e.g. animal research, the development of new theories and terminology, education to emerging problems, the manufacture and consumption of new products) to mask the illusory quality of the goal. The 'longer life span' which is ripped out of the cycle of Nature is not an affirmation of life but rather a denial of it. The violent acts legitimated in pursuit of longevity reveal the *quest* for what it is – the *conquest* of Nature and the body. Couching these acts in terms of 'progress', 'sensitivity to the elderly', 'compassion', 'human welfare' . . . further obscures their underlying violence and deadly intent.

The paradox of prolonging life by destroying it is embedded in animal experimentation. So long as 'new results' keep feeding the treadmill, the non-search continues unhampered by the truth. And the truth is that animals suffer and die to produce those results which presumably will enable scientists to keep human bodies running with spare parts (organ transplants), boosted fuels (biological fuel cells, drugs and endocrine gland manipulations), electronic hook-ups (cybernetics) and a general tinkering with body cells. 'Freezing' live bodies to be resuscitated at a later time is an experimental technique aimed at immortality (*à la* Rip Van Winkle) and is also a word that aptly captures the climate of this whole enterprise. It is clear that the view of longevity that guides this research belongs to the larger object-ification pattern whereby nature is first reduced/impoverished/

mechanised and then replaced with 'improved' synthetic parts.

Man's concept of longevity/immortality is a devastating myth that debilitates by creating dependencies on Father (scientists, media-makers, doctors . . .). Research on longevity is a sterile search, made the more ironic by the omnipresent threat to life which man in his arrogant possession of the earth has spread all over the universe. If indeed there is a 'key' to longevity, it will not be found in the slicing of animal cells, tissue, genes or brains but rather in the relinquishing of the grip man has over all that lives, and in our re-fusing his longevity with unqualified living.

Freeing the animals

> Do we fully understand that we aim at nothing less
> than an entire subversion of the present order of
> society, a dissolution of the whole existing social
> compact?

> Elizabeth Oakes Smith, 'A Dissolution of the
> Existing Social Compact', 1852

Imagine that aliens endowed with a man-like mentality invaded Earth in search of experimental subjects. Suppose they held life in contempt and humans as barely sentient, inferior creatures, excellent specimens in fact to serve as animated instruments and living tools in their vast and various health projects. They want to help themselves. They want information to feed into their new technologies. They dream of conquering space. They do not question the morality of capturing humans. They do not hesitate to cage and torture us, cement all kinds of hardware into us, wire us to super-electronic machines, reward and punish us to modify our behaviour, infect us with diseases unknown to us. We resist. We reason. We bite, punch, kick, scream, pound, scratch, pull and tug to exhaustion. We are restrained in harnesses. We are sedated by force. We are exterminated. We go down in their history books as vicious, stupid, dangerous, uncooperative. We are indeed inferior. They can prove it.

In 'Beaver Tears', Dr Alice B. Sheldon (writing under the pseudonym of James Tiptree, Jr) imagines a similar scenario. Her story describes a man watching a nature show on television about the relocation of beavers. He falls asleep. He wakes up to find himself in the same predicament as the trapped beavers, bruised, separated from his wife and child, and utterly bewildered. He realises that he and a handful of neighbours have been captured by aliens and are aboard a spaceship bound for an unknown destination. As he recognises and observes his cagemates, he concludes that the relocation of their future human colony promises no change from those necrophilic values and violent behaviour that prevail on planet Earth.[85]

In 1979 I spoke about the human harassment of animals at a symposium organised to protest against the harassment of feminist professors in American universities. After the lecture, a visibly upset woman in the audience rose and demanded that we all march to the research laboratories of Harvard University, where she had previously been employed. We would open the doors to all the cages. We would free the animals. Our example would motivate women all over the world to take all research laboratories by storm and this would be the end of the animals' concentration/extermination-camp existence everywhere. We all remained in our seats. I drove home feeling like a hypocrite and rationalised our powerlessness.

My fantasies run the same course as those of that admirable woman. I see huge numbers of women taking over all the laboratories in the world. I see euthanasia for the hopelessly maimed and I see freedom. I see teams upon teams of researchers pace the empty floors and hear echoes, stare at the blank walls and face their shattered illusions. Let them ponder what they have done. I also see each and every one doing what she does best. For some, this best is marching on laboratories. Others will choose the power of the spoken/written word. All will choose to refuse participation in man's brutal treatment of life, in whatever shape it is manifested.

Women can readily identify with the plight of animals, not only because we are so closely of nature but also and primarily because we recognise the many faces of oppression. We react to them in every fibre of our being. We can be moved to outrage without feeling a need to justify our emotions. I felt profoundly irritated by Peter Singer's insistence on being *reasonable* about his opposition to the abuse of animals, even though *Animal Liberation: A New Ethics for our Treatment of Animals* is a courageous book that needed to be written, and even though I agree with the proposition that animal experimentation

and intensive farming are 'morally unjustifiable' and 'morally repugnant'. Singer's fear of appearing too 'soft', of being called 'an animal
lover' and appealing to emotions 'that cannot be supported by reason'
limits his analysis of the connection between speciesism and sexism.

First, take 'liberation': it is the wrong word to use with reference to
animals, if only by virtue of the associations that have accrued to it.
True liberation movements* have always started from among the oppressed and have been fuelled by anger, frustration, and yearning to
be free. The Black Liberation and the Women's Liberation
Movements (as earlier the Abolitionist Movement) are waves of oppressed people moving to liberate themselves from the oppressor's
grip *and* from the internalised perception of the self as victim which
keeps the oppressed bound to the oppressor. Liberation is an individual's personal exorcism of the enemy within as well as that individual's battle with the pressures of culture, prejudice, and oppression. Animals have no such battle to fight. All they need is freedom
from human control.

Peter Singer and many who have written on behalf of freeing the
animals – I think especially of Richard Ryder, Brigid Brophy, and
some of the more perceptive contributors to *Animals*, the publication
of the Massachusetts Society for the Prevention of Cruelty to
Animals – are aware of these connections but leave too much unsaid.
Still, on the speciesist front alone, we face a challenge. As Singer put
it, the choice is between tyranny and altruism:

> . . . Will we rise to the challenge and prove our capacity for genuine
> altruism by ending our ruthless exploitation of the species in our power,
> not because we are forced to do so by rebels or terrorists, but because we
> recognize that our position is morally indefensible?
> The way in which we answer this question depends on the way in which
> each one of us, individually, answers it.[86]

In addition to Singer's suggestions for action – vegetarianism,
careful consumption of manufactured 'goods', letter-writing to
representatives, public figures, exploitative companies, etc. – I

---

* A false liberation movement is that which starts at the top and
manipulates the masses with the promise of freedom. False liberation
movements are oppressively patronising (China, Russia, Cuba) as they
merely replace one form of patriarchal rule by another.

suggest that we ought to aim for a redirection of all the monies lavished on subsidising laboratory research into finding ways to decontaminate the Earth and its atmosphere from harmful pollutants without using animals. The monies poured into the manufacture of food additives, cosmetics, plastics, and endless new chemicals, for endless new uses, should be channelled into banning all such products. Thrown back on their own resources, the scientists would be forced to think of alternative methods or careers.

Ultimately and realistically, the responsibility lies with individuals to seek a wholesome way of life and liberate themselves from fears, prejudices, and misconceptions – superstitions all, of man's enfevered civilisation, enfeebled imagination and purposeful amnesia. Women especially must do some serious thinking and reconnect, if not to our gynocentric roots, at the very least to the history of man's violence to animals. For what has been done to animals has always preceded what has been done to us.

Notes

1. Aristotle, 'Ethica Nicomachea', in Richard McKeon (ed.), *Introduction to Aristotle* (New York: The Modern Library, Inc., 1947), p.488.
2. Quoted in Floyd W. Matson, *The Broken Image: Man, Science and Society* (New York: George Braziller, Inc., 1964), p.64.
3. W. Lane-Petter (ed.), *Animals for Research: Principles of Breeding and Management* (London: Academic Press, 1963), pp.vii–viii.
4. Vance Packard, *The People Shapers* (New York: Bantam Books, Inc., 1977; London: Macdonald & Jane's, 1978), pp.409–15.
5. Quoted in Peter Singer, *Animal Liberation: A New Ethics for our Treatment of Animals* (New York: Avon Books, 1975; London: Jonathan Cape, 1976), pp.62–3.
6. John C. Lilly, *Lilly on Dolphins: Humans of the Sea* (New York: Anchor Books Edition, 1975), p.28.
7. ibid., p.27.
8. Quoted in R.A. McCance, 'Perinatal physiology', in A.L. Hodgkin *et al.*, *The Pursuit of Nature: Informal Essays on the History of Physiology* (Cambridge: Cambridge University Press, 1979), p.134.
9. By a curious twist of double think, the word 'subject' can refer both to the doer of an act (the agent) and to the *object* of the agent's deed. We can say, 'The experimenter burned the subject (animal)', or again,

'Subject 1 pushed Subject 2 against the cage', with the tacit understanding of who is doing what to whom. Grammatically speaking, we say that 'experimenter' is the subject of the first sentence while 'subject' is the direct *object*. In the second sentence, one 'subject' is an agent who has acted upon another 'subject' who is now the *object* of the sentence. This ambivalent use of the word suggests an ontological perception of the self as servant, even as victim, as in 'God's subjects', 'the Queen's/King's subjects', 'subject to Fate', 'subject to time', 'subject to approval', or the passive form of the verb, 'to be subjected to'. Even the etymology of the word (sub-ject, to throw under) bears this out.

10. See H.R. Hays, *Birds, Beasts and Men* (New York: G.P. Putnam's Sons, 1972; London: J.M. Dent, 1973) p.240, where Hays attributes Bernard's wife's objections to his work to fanatic religiosity and bigotry.

11. Ivan P. Pavlov, *Conditioned Reflexes: An Investigation of the Physiological Activity of the Cerebral Cortex*, trans. and ed. by G.V. Anrep (New York: Dover Publications, Inc., 1960), p.411.

12. ibid., p.287.

13. Ronald Melzack and T.H. Scott, 'The effects of early experience on the response to pain', *Journal of Comparative and Physiological Psychology*, 50 (1957), p.158.

14. ibid., p.159.

15. ibid.

16. ibid., p.160.

17. Joan McIntyre, 'Mind in the waters', in Joan McIntyre (assembler), *Mind in the Waters* (New York: Charles Scribner's Sons, 1974), p.222.

18. Andrea Dworkin, *Pornography: Men Possessing Women* (New York: Perigee Books, 1981; London: The Women's Press, 1981), p.74.

19. Quoted in Dworkin, *Pornography: Men Possessing Women*, p.91.

20. For a discussion of MacLean's view of the ultimate cause of human violence, see Chapter 2, pp.38-9.

21. Paul D. MacLean, 'Man's reptilian and limbic inheritance', in T.J. Boag and D. Campbell (eds.), *A Triune Concept of the Brain and Behavior* (Toronto: University of Toronto Press, 1973), p.16.

22. ibid., p.18. It is illuminating to contrast the *reality* of what MacLean and his colleagues are doing to animals, and the reasons they offer for doing it, with the image of him presented in *Science Digest* as a thoughtful, sensitive man who is deeply committed to humanitarian concerns. He said: 'What is so unusual about human beings is that we've developed this curious concern, not only for ourselves but for other living things. . . . For God's sake, what are we doing here? Why is there so much pain and anguish, so much suffering?' (Quoted in Mary Long, 'Ritual and deceit', *Science Digest*, November/December 1980, p.121.)

23. Sigmund Freud, *Civilization and its Discontents*, trans. and ed. by James Strachey (New York: W.W. Norton and Company, Inc., 1962; London: Hogarth Press, 1963), pp.38–9.
24. Quoted in José M.R. Delgado, *Physical Control of the Mind: Toward a Psychocivilized Society* (New York: Harper & Row, 1969), p.xix.
25. Jean Rostand, *Humanly Possible: A Biologist's Notes on the Future of Mankind*, trans. by Lowell Bair (New York: Saturday Review Press, 1973), p.153.
26. Delgado, *Physical Control of the Mind*, p.101.
27. Singer, *Animal Liberation: A New Ethics for our Treatment of Animals*, p.34.
28. Quoted in David F. Salisbury, 'Animals in the laboratory: a necessary cruelty?', *The Christian Science Monitor* (9 March 1978), p.14.
29. It would take volumes to compile all such experiments conducted in this country alone every year. In1978, it was estimated that 64 million animals were being used every year in experiments that involve intense suffering (see Patricia Curtis, 'New debate over experimenting with animals', *The New York Times Magazine*, 31 December 1978, p.23). There is every reason to believe that the count is increasing. Although mice, rats, cats, and dogs are the animals most frequently used in laboratories – and most frequently objectified in a cutesy and trivial sort of way: Mickey Mouse, Felix the Cat, Snoopy, etc. – hardly a species is left that has not shed its blood and/or contributed its pain for what *Es* like to call 'human welfare'.
30. For an 'even-handed' review and discussion of this issue see D.H. Smyth, *Alternatives to Animal Experiments* (London: Scolar Press, 1978). Smyth, a physiologist and an experimenter, was commissioned to write his book by the Research Defence Society of England. He regards himself, in his words, 'as an animal lover' who accepts the 'use [of] animals for food, for clothing, for companionship, for sport, for medical and veterinary research, and for many other purposes, but in assuming *this right* we also have the gravest responsibility not to cause any unnecessary suffering to any living creature' (emphasis added), pp.210–11. In short, he is a good example of a scientist who conscientiously practises his god-given *right* to objectify animals – whether in the laboratory or at home – and to treat them as the situation allows, seemingly unaware that his reservations do not erase the immorality of all animal experimentation.
31. Lois Kaplan, 'Collard attacks', *The Justice* (10 March 1981), p.2.
32. Smyth, *Alternatives to Animal Experiments*, p.81.
33. Richard D. Ryder, *Victims of Science: The Use of Animals in Research* (London: Davis-Poynter, 1975), p.17.
34. Lane-Petter (ed.) *Animals for Research*, p.viii.

35. Thus Paul MacLean assures his readers that satisfying the neocortex consists of gearing up to keep pace with rocket-speed transportation while the limbic system, requiring the pace of the horse and buggy, can be 'calmed' living the way Europeans live: 'a little smell of horse manure each week' goes a long way in 'quieting something deep down inside', and learning the value of 'creating pictures and other things'. (See MacLean, 'Man's reptilian and limbic inheritance', pp.15–16.)

36. Joan McIntyre, 'Iceberg', in McIntyre (assembler), *Mind in the Waters*, p.107.

37. Karen De Witt, 'A company that thrives on regulation', *The New York Times* (7 December 1980), p.F-9. In 1984 Bausch and Lomb Inc, the maker of contact lenses, acquired Charles River Breeding Laboratories in a stock swap valued at just under 135 million dollars.

38. Advertisement in *Laboratory Animal Science* 29, (1) (February 1979), p.20.

39. Herein lies another parallel between the treatment of nature, animals and women in patriarchal cultures. For a detailed account of the variety of procurement methods in the prostitution trade, see Kathleen Barry, *Female Sexual Slavery* (New Jersey: Prentice Hall, Inc., 1979), pp.73-96.

40. Quoted in Curtis, 'New debate over experimenting with animals', p.21. In that same year, Henry Foster began breeding rhesus monkeys on Florida's Key Lois and Key Racoon.

41. Henry L. Foster, 'Specific pathogen-free animals', in Lane-Petter (ed.), *Animals for Research*. pp.111-12.

42. ibid., p.114.

43. ibid., p.114.

44. ibid., p.113.

45. Gena Corea, *The Hidden Malpractice: How American Medicine Mistreats Women* (New York: Jove Publications, Inc., 1978), p.224.

46. ibid., p.209.

47. Foster, 'Specific pathogen-free animals', p.137.

48. Curtis, 'New debate over experimenting with animals', pp.21 and 23.

49. Singer, *Animal Liberation: A New Ethics for our Treatment of Animals*, pp.49-50.

50. June Weir, 'High-tech faces', *The New York Times Magazine* (29 July 1984), p.37.

51. ibid., p.37.

52. During the EDB crisis – ethylene dibromide (EDB) is a pesticide and fumigant used on grain, fruit, and vegetables both in the field and in storage – shoppers interviewed in supermarkets said they were neither worried nor upset and would not change their buying habits. This is an admittedly small, non-random sample of consumers. Yet obviously most

people continue to buy products which are covered with herbicide and pesticide residues and are pumped with additives and preservatives. If they refused to buy them, these products would not be stocked in supermarkets. And this is the case even though a January 1984 poll of American consumers conducted by the Food Marketing Institute showed that 77 per cent reported they viewed those residues as a 'serious hazard' and 32 per cent also considered additives and preservatives as dangerous (*Not Man Apart: The Newsmagazine of Friends of the Earth*, 14 (4) (May 1984), p.3). They are informed. They express grave concern. They continue to consume.

53. This contrast is highlighted by the offerings of supermarkets which allocate very little space to 'fresh' produce – an aisle or two tucked away in a far end of the store – but overwhelm consumers with aisle upon aisle of processed foods, junk foods and other manufactured products. Even so, there is no connection between the produce arranged cosmetically to catch the shopper's eye and the environment in which real fruit and vegetables grow. In the same way, cuts of meat wrapped in plastic are dissociated entirely from animals.

54. Few and short-lived. According to Dr Terry A. Tattar, professor of plant pathology at the University of Massachusetts, Amherst, the average life-span of a tree in a US city is seventeen years. (See *Garden Clippings: Horticultural Newsletter*, Cooperative Extension Service, University of Massachusetts, Nov.-Dec. 1986, 6, (10), p.3).

55. Quoted in 'Answering your questions about CANCER' (American Cancer Society, Inc., National Headquarters, 219 E. 42nd St, New York, 1976), p.6.

56. Mary Daly, *Pure Lust: Elemental Feminist Philosophy* (Boston, Mass.: Beacon Press, 1984; London: The Women's Press, 1984), pp.122–52.

57. Philip M. Boffey, 'New findings about cancer raising hope', *The New York Times*, 20 February 1983, p.1.

58. Dr V.T. DeVita, Jr, director of the National Cancer Institute (a Federal agency) who expects to use $46 million to support cancer gene research in 1984, was quoted as making this comment in Boffey, op.cit., p.30.

59. Quoted ibid.

60. Quoted in 'New cancer clue', *The New York Times: Other Issues and Trends* (1 April 1979).

61. A 1984 study of California-grown produce by the National Resources Defense Council uncovered 19 pesticide residues, including DDT, in a sample of 13 vegetables and fruits. Eight of the 19 are suspected of causing cancer. Michael LaFavore, 'Unseen additives', *Organic Gardening* (July 1984), pp.65–8.

62. Quoted ibid., p.66.

63. 'Carcinogenicity testing is of particular importance for food additives

to be used in the United States, as the "Delaney Clause" in the Federal Food, Drugs and Cosmetics Act of 1962 excludes from food, even in the smallest concentration, any substance which has ever been found to be carcinogenic even in the highest concentration.' Smyth, *Alternatives to Animal Experiments*, p.70.

64. Quoted in J. Tevere MacFadyen, 'Behind the natural-foods facade', *Country Journal* (August 1984), p.40.

65. ibid.

66. J. Bruce Overmier and Martin E.P. Seligman, 'Effects of inescapable shock upon subsequent escape and avoidance responding', *Journal of Comparative and Physiological Psychology*, 63 (1) (1967), p.28.

67. Reported in Singer, *Animal Liberation: A New Ethics for our Treatment of Animals*, p.43.

68. Jay M. Weiss *et al.*, 'Neurotransmitters and helplessness: a chemical bridge to depression?', *Psychology Today* (December 1974), p.62.

69. Delgado, *Physical Control of the Mind*, p.174.

70. ibid., p.36.

71. Elliot S. Valenstein, *Brain Control: A Critical Examination of Brain Stimulation and Psychosurgery* (New York: John Wiley & Sons, 1973; Chichester: John Wiley & Sons, 1974), p.61.

72. ibid., p.73.

73. Samuel Corson, E. O'Leary Corson, Eugene Arnold and Walter Knopp, 'Animal models of violence and hyperkinesis: Interaction of psychopharmacologic and psychosocial therapy in behavior modification', in George Serban and Arthur Kling (eds.), *Animal Models in Human Psychobiology* (New York: Plenum Press, 1976), p.121.

74. Anne Cameron, *Daughters of Copper Woman* (Vancouver: Press Gang Publishers, 1981; London: The Women's Press, 1984), p.145.

75. Delgado, *Physical Control of the Mind*, pp.4–5.

76. For critical exposés see David Rorvik, *As Man Becomes Machine* (New York: Pocket Books, 1978; London: Souvenir Press, 1973); Theodore Roszak, *Where the Wasteland Ends* (New York: Doubleday, 1972; London: Faber & Faber, 1973): Vance Packard, *The People Shapers* (New York: Bantam Books, Inc., 1977); and David Rorvik, *In His Image: The Cloning of Man* (New York: Pocket Books, 1978; London: Hamish Hamilton, 1978).

77. Delgado, *Physical Control of the Mind*, p.223.

78. Quoted in Nigel Calder, *The Mind of Man* (New York: Viking Press, 1971; London: BBC Publications, 1970), p.274.

79. Daly, *Pure Lust*, pp.339–40 and 362–3.

80. Jules H. Masserman, 'Unpredictability in the etiology of behavioral deviations', in Serban and Kling (eds.), *Animal Models in Human Psychobiology*, p.107.

81. Daly, *Pure Lust*, p.98.
82. Bernard W. Agranoff, 'Memory and protein synthesis', in Richard F. Thompson (Introduction), *Physiological Psychology: Readings from 'Scientific American'* (San Francisco: W.H. Freeman & Company, 1971), p.380.
83. The ability to erase or prevent the formation of memories has tremendous political as well as personal implications. Reportedly when Agranoff was asked whether the Central Intelligence Agency had contacted him concerning his work, he replied with a smile, 'I forget'. Gordon Rattray Taylor, *The Biological Time Bomb* (New York: Mentor Books, 1969; London: Thames & Hudson, 1968), p.141.
84. Kady, *The double axe is the sign of the Goddess* (Iowa City Women's Press, July 1984). In this connection I want to mention the yet unpublished work of photographer Diana Davies of Northampton, Massachusetts, who has assembled an impressive collection of Goddess images from around the world, and whose vision of the Goddess has guided her also to photograph strong women leading strong lives.
85. James Tiptree, Jr, 'Beaver Tears', in *Out of the Everywhere and Other Extraordinary Visions* (New York: Ballantine Books, 1981), pp.28–33.
86. Singer, *Animal Liberation: A New Ethics for our Treatment of Animals*, p.258.

4. Life with father

The rot of masculist materialism has indeed
permeated all spheres of twentieth-century life and
now attacks its very core.

Elizabeth Gould Davis, *The First Sex*

The catalogue of scientific vice is familiar: it
duplicates, exaggerates, the catalogue of 'male' vices
in general.

Shulamith Firestone, *The Dialectic of Sex: The Case
for Feminist Revolution*

Toute l'activité masculine n'est qu'une énorme
névrose collective. (All masculine activity is but an
enormous collective neurosis.)

Evelyne Sullerot, *Droit de Regard*

You want us to act like you, to be like you so that we
will be more acceptable, more likeable. You should
try to be more like us regarding communal coexistence; respect and care for all living things and
for the earth, the waters, and the atmosphere; respect
for human dignity and the right to be who they are.

Carol Lee Sanchez, Native American, 'Sex, class
and race intersections: visions of women of color'·
Sinister Wisdom, 22/23

As for turning things into objects: Isn't that the principal source of violence? The fetishizing of vital, contradictory people and processes, within public notifications, until they have rigidified into ready-made parts and stage scenery: dead themselves, killing others.

Christa Wolf, Cassandra

Divine intervention

To be men, we must be in control. That is the first and the last ethical word.

Joseph Fletcher, Professor of Medical Ethics, 'Ethical aspects of genetic controls', New England Journal of Medicine

I propose that the core of sadism, common to all its manifestations, is *the passion to have absolute control over a living being*, whether an animal, a child, a man, or a woman. (emphasis added)

Eric Fromm, The Anatomy of Human Destructiveness

Nothing links the human animal and nature so profoundly as woman's reproductive system which enables her to share the experience of bringing forth and nourishing life with the rest of the living world. *Whether or not she personally experiences biological mothering*, it is in this that woman is most truly a child of nature and in this natural integrity lies the wellspring of her strength.

Under patriarchy, woman's strength is reversed and her natural integrity negated. The deep fear that motivates this oppression is the patriarch's fear of female autonomy, the enemy within, which must be held in check by compulsory heterosexuality and compulsory fertility. Required to yield and defer to man's wishes, a woman is valued for her capacity to bear her *husband's sons*. (Neither the child nor female fertility are valued for themselves but as tokens of male virility and control of female autonomy. This is clear when one considers the shame cast upon a woman who bears a child out of wedlock, shame which reflects upon the child. The one exception concerns the use of surrogate mothers only because the husbands have given their consent and the surrogate relinquishes the child to the father.)* Producing sons is a source of status and rivalry among women as well as a condition for winning man's approval, perhaps even his 'love'. In the Book of Genesis, 'Rachel, seeing that she herself gave Jacob no children, became jealous of her sister [Leah, who had given him four sons]. And she said to Jacob, "Give me children, or I shall die!"' (30:1-2).[1] These women despair at barrenness because their value, not only to the patriarch but to other women as well, lies in replicating the male. In a statement that foreshadows modern surgical interventions into the female reproductive system, Leah and Rachel acknowledge their gratitude to Yahweh for having 'opened their womb[s]', thereby giving Leah a chance to win her husband's 'love' and taking away Rachel's shame. Apparently neither one had her expectations met since two more sons later Leah repeats 'this time my husband will be united to me, for I have now borne three sons to him', (29:34) and Rachel pleads, 'May Yahweh give me another son!' (30:24). Pitted against each other in fierce competition to produce more and more sons for Jacob ('I have fought God's fight with my sister' (30:8)), each woman gives her slave as a surrogate mother for Jacob's seed. Both surrogates bear sons. Leah exclaims, 'What happiness! Women will call me happy!' (30:13).

* Throughout this chapter, references to 'surrogates' and 'surrogate mothers' have been used in the popular sense of the woman/female who 'stands in place of' another woman/female who is unable (not allowed, in the case of animals) to carry offspring to term. Since the writing of this chapter and the death of Andrée Collard, I have come across an excellent discussion of surrogacy by Katha Pollitt ('The strange case of Baby M', *The Nation*, 23 May 1987, pp.667–88) which leads me to revise my original understanding and use of the term. As Pollitt affirms, correctly, in my view, '"Mother" describes the relationship of a woman to a child, not to the father of that child and his wife . . . If anyone [is] a surrogate, it [is] the one who substitute[s], or wish[es] to substitute, for the child's *actual* mother' (p.682, emphasis added). On the other hand, Andrée Collard included in the reality of 'mother' the notions of *informed* and *willing* impregnation, gestation, delivery and maternal responsibility. In an earlier version of chapter 4, she wrote 'women impregnated by rape (in the marital bed or elsewhere) and denied abortion, and human surrogates are not mothers and neither are the women dependent on having children for status in the eyes of the male.' The reader is advised to keep these important distinctions in mind when reading chapter 4 [collaborator's note].

This language of futility and despair is tame by comparison with the emotional language that today surrounds infertility. Women are manipulated to fear barrenness as 'the cruel and unyielding enemy', 'the saddest epidemic' which 'rips at the core of the [heterosexual] couple's relationship', damaging 'sexuality, self-image, and self-esteem'.[2] Alienated from her Self by centuries of conditioned dependency, the male-identified woman accepts man's definition of her sexuality, image and esteem. Without his approval, she falls prey to meaninglessness and she panics. When woman loses contact with her inherent meaning[3] she can perceive all birthing experiences as equal, regardless of the kind and the degree of technological intervention which brings about these births.

In this setting, the scientist looms like a magician on woman's horizon. She has been prepared to allow the experts' manipulations into the intimate confines of her body and mind, just as the Trojans, tired of a long siege and caught off guard, accepted within their walls the treacherous gift horse that spelled their doom.[4] The scientists' gift[5] of life is presented with a paraphernalia of hormonal stimulants, *Playboy* magazines to stimulate ejaculation in the man, petri dishes, ultrasound monitors, laparoscopes, laser surgery, etc. It contains the poison that ensures the death of woman's link to nature. She becomes a mere babymaking machine, regardless of whether she is the donor of egg or embryo, the recipient of embryo (*in vitro* fertilisation) or sperm (artificial insemination), or the noncontributing, passive observer of her surrogate. In the realm of life with father, she is pronounced normal and blessed. Like Leah, she is happy among women. Temporarily she has managed to dispel the castration fears of the fathers and to deflect their hostility by surrendering her womb into their hands. It is no wonder that the 'Army of God' (a militant 'pro-life' group in the United States) bombs abortion clinics while leaving these reproductive centres unscathed.

The 'life engineers' take control of the female creative processes ostensibly to help humanity in distress. In reality they seek to control all species by restructuring them along strictly utilitarian lines, that is, as products which the dominant white male in politically dominant countries has determined as being useful and profitable to him. In the process, they will eliminate not only biological motherhood but most women as well. As Gena Corea correctly concludes after documenting and discussing the widespread gynocidal implementation of sex-predetermination techniques/technologies, 'If many women in the Third World are eliminated through sex predetermination, if fewer firstborn females exist throughout the world, if the percentages of poor women and richer men rise in the overdeveloped nations, then it is indeed gynicide we are discussing.'[6]

The bioengineers are obviously not concerned about human welfare, let alone the welfare of women. According to the CBS report of 30 October 1979 entitled 'The Baby Makers', a team of biochemical engineers in a Calcutta public hospital, working with funds allocated to improve birth control programmes, removed and froze the embryos from the wombs of one hundred women 'donors', later implanting them in the wombs of one hundred recipient women. Unconcerned about the welfare of these women, they were equally unconcerned about the defects and abnormalities they might have been producing. According to the Chief of Operations there, 'We were not really worried about genetic abnormalities. We would rather have had an abnormal baby than no baby at all.'

The report showed the rivalry and intense competition that pervade genetic research and make scientists 'cut corners in order to win the race'. They thereby receive, just as the Calcutta group received, 'congratulations by the thousands of scientists' from all over the world, 'and no adverse criticism at all.' 'Thousands of scientists' voiced 'no adverse criticism at all.' This statement indicates that the Calcutta experiment was not exceptional but widespread. It also shows a deliberate attempt to deceive. Among themselves, a cutthroat competition that allows any and all violations of life. For the outside, a uniform message of benevolence and concern for life.

Reproductive technologies are still in their experimental stage. The need of human subjects is critical. In western countries, women cannot be forced to submit to these violations, so first they must be conditioned into accepting them. Therefore, the need to enlist the agencies of control (business, industry, government, education) is critical in 'engineering voter approval', as Vance Packard called the campaigns of persuasion that are taking place worldwide. In her insightful discussion, 'Informed consent: the myth of voluntarism', Gena Corea exposes the silences, half-truths, and emotional manipulations to which the consenting victims of these experiments are subjected.[7] Needless to say, truth is hardly ever allowed to surface in the media since the stake is to make the loss of nature and woman appear not only necessary but desirable.

The reproduction of barrenness

The loss of nature and woman involves matricide, or the killing of the mother principle in life-cycles and processes, rendering them impossible without technological assistance. This loss is irreversible. For instance, a cow that has been injected with hormones so that she generates dozens of calves a year without birthing any of them is a superovulator who needs surrogate cows and a great deal of reproductive technology in order for the life process begun in her to come to fruition. In this case, the cow is alive and can still be used but the mother in her has been killed. To take another example, soil that has been forced to yield beyond its natural capacity through the use of superseeds and chemical fertility is made barren. Viability must then be achieved either through the use of more chemicals and super superseeds or by the replacement of the soil itself, as is the case with hydroponic culture. The soil is still there to be trod upon (in the former instance), but Mother Earth has been killed. Or again, chickens that are transformed into super egg-producers through hormonal and genetic interferences cannot bring life into being. Their eggs are infertile and their natural brooding instinct has been bred out. Although the chicken is alive for X number of days and lays far too many eggs, the mother-hen in her has been killed. The cow, the soil, the hen have been rendered incapable of bringing forth life on their own. They have become artificially (by the work of man) infertile. (I mention the cow, the earth, and the chicken for their long symbolic association with women. The cow was a major sacred animal in many ancient gynocentric societies. She is usually intimately related to the Moon and represents nurturance as well as fertility. The association of women and chickens is more recent. It is pejorative.)

Artificial infertility kills the autonomy of female being as surely as artificial fertility. Both are interdependent aspects of the same attempt to control production and reproduction. The basic condition of man-made infertility underlying 'high-yield', 'high productivity', is obscured by the emphasis on the marvels of technology which supposedly can remedy the problems of feeding an overpopulated, hungry world by the production of enormous quantities of inexpensive meat, eggs, grains, vegetables. However, the use of superseeds and super-ovulators in food production translates inevitably into a drastic reduction of viable life.

The real issue, although it is skilfully disguised in the self-deceptive reversals of Orwellian double-think,[8] is the concerted effort to bring about universal barrenness within which selected areas/individuals will be cultivated for specialised breeding. This is already clear in the area of food production of which the plight of American farmers is an example. Facing bankruptcy as a result of expensive loans (to finance expensive machinery, seeds, pesticides, fertilisers), farmers are victims of the overall plan to consolidate huge tracts of land under multinational corporate ownership/control, thus regulating production and 'freeing' agricultural soil for development.[9] Farmland, which is already besieged by air and water pollution from industrialised areas as well as from modern agricultural practices, is eroding at the rate of 25.4 billion tons a year worldwide. This compounds the dependency on superseeds, monocropping, the use of man-made chemicals, financing and government aid. The net result is increased infertility. The threat of world famine which this artificial (man-made) infertility poses is then used to legitimate control of productivity and reproductivity through land consolidation and ownership by the powerful few as well as increased dependence on (lethal) technology.

The same syndrome affects cattle ranching, dairy farming and the production of fruit and vegetables. Again, individual operators are being forced out of business in order to intensify corporate centres in which the 'newest' technology controls the quantity, quality, and distribution of products meted out to 'special' populations, largely affluent whites. Under these practices, plant and animal fertility is restricted to a determined number of superproducts dependent on the technology for their ability to yield. The others are then culled or put to various uses, whichever suits the controllers' purposes.

It is common knowledge that the natural gene pool in plant and animal life – wild and domesticated – has been reduced as a result of species extinction (man-made) or deliberate selection by 'seedsmen' and animal breeders. Moreover, genetic as well as growth and biological-time manipulations of the remaining species is taking away their natural reproductive ability, as in the case of chickens. Artificial insemination and genetic engineering of cattle have made some females, if not infertile, utterly dependent on man's controlling technology. The same is true of vegetative hybrids and animal crosses[10] which are incapable of reproduction.

Human infertility is also on the rise. Digging a little deeper into this 'saddest of epidemics' it is clear that the tripling of the American infertility rate in the past twenty years is merely a *symptom* of the real epidemic which is the patriarchal lust for power and control over life. For women infertility most commonly results from a blockage or abnormality of the Fallopian tubes. The scarring of the delicate tissues of a woman's reproductive system is most often caused by pelvic inflammatory disease (PID) resulting from intrauterine devices used to prevent conception and from the venereal diseases, chlamydia and gonorrhoea. Venereal disease is supposedly increasing among women because of 'liberated sexual attitudes'.[11]

Many women have noticed that the sexual liberation granted to us in the 1960s by men is just another means to control female sexuality. Before, women adhering to the double standard of female asexuality/male sexuality could not say 'yes': now, under the standard of sexual permissiveness, women cannot say 'no'. (Of course married women have never been allowed to say 'no'. Rape of a woman by her husband is still considered by many a *logical* impossibility.) Sexual activity has become a male expectation in heterosexual encounters ranging from casual to intimate. Women who refuse run a high risk of being coerced emotionally and/or physically to submit.[12] The male-defined 'gift' of sexuality ultimately contains our infertility, to overcome which we must accept another of his gifts – his reproductive technologies.

Recently 'the blame for childless marriages' has been extended to male deficiencies which are the cause 40–50 per cent of the time.[13] The most common diagnosis of the man's problem is low sperm count and this is increasingly linked to the proliferation of toxic chemicals in the environment and in the groundwater over the past fifty years. Some 'genotoxins' have been isolated at 'alarmingly high levels' in semen: DDT, polychlorinated biphenyls (PCBs), hexachlorobenzene, pentachlorophenol, and Tris, the government-mandated flame retardant added to fabrics before it was recognised as a carcinogen.[14] Other pesticides, herbicides and common industrial chemicals known to be genotoxic and/or carcinogenic are still in use, even if that use has been limited by EPA 'bans'. Other banned genotoxins, such as dioxin (Agent Orange), are being released in increasing amounts into the atmosphere as by-products of the combustion of plastics in many city dumps.[15] As one genotoxin is banned or restricted, others rise up or appear from different sources. Even if completely eliminated, those already produced persist in the environment in concentrations which increase at each 'higher' position in the food chain – ending with humans. Therefore, there is no reason to suspect that male infertility will be reversed except through dependency on reproductive technologies.

As for carrying a child to term and birthing it, already few women in Western industrialised countries feel able to do so without relying on a battery of pre-natal tests, hospital delivery, and post-natal care. 'Health' is the superfetish that compels them to this dependency by tapping the fear of uncertainty that pervades the culture but specifically in this case, the fear of birth defects, congenital disease, 'complications', and so on.

These fears are implanted and fostered by doctors who are trained to perceive pregnancy as a 'deeply dangerous medical condition' fraught with possibilities of serious life-threatening problems for both mother and baby, all requiring quick medical, technological intervention. They define a normal birth as a 'negative event' – one with the fortuitous absence of complications.[16] In turn, doctors instil in their 'patients' a morbid fear of pathology, a sense of female inadequacy and ignorance and a blind dependency on the doctor–saviour. These attitudes and efforts on the part of obstetricians to control the birth process were stepped up during the 1970s – the decade of the second wave of the Women's Movement. The movement was paralleled by an increase in the rate of Caesarean sections in the United States from 4.5 per 100 births in 1965 to 19 per 100 births in 1982.

When a woman accepts her doctor's definition of pregnancy and childbirth as exclusively 'medical events' she subverts her faith in herself and in her normal body processes. Should she resist and insist that her body processes are normal and trustworthy by refusing tests and a 'high-tech' hospital birth, she must face the disapproval and the ultimate 'blame' if anything 'goes wrong'. As one woman who gave birth to her child at home put it: 'You have to accept that if anything goes wrong – even if it's something that would have gone wrong in a hospital, even if it's something like a birth defect – if you have the baby at home, everyone will blame you.'[17] Not surprisingly, only about 2 per cent of women in the United States currently give birth at home.

Keeping these consolidating trends in mind, together with the concepts of selectivity, controlled production, and the customary application to humans of research done routinely on laboratory and farm animals, it is clear to me that infertility is the overall design. Only 'special' women would be allowed to continue to breed while the rest of us would gradually be phased out. However, this too is but a step toward the elimination not only of women, but of all other species as we know them, including our own.

We live in the transitional period in which every woman's choice is crucial. Human reproductive technology is no longer a question of feasibility: it is a question of the total acceptance or total rejection of it. Looking at it as an isolated phenomenon is taking the piecemeal approach that further fragments, therefore blinds and allows the implementation of abusive techniques in other segments of life. It helps nothing at all to focus on starvation in Ethiopia while the industrial countries gorge themselves, producing wastes that could feed the continents they lay to waste instead. Likewise, it is futile to debate the morality of, and caution against the abuse of, artificial fertility without taking into account the undermining of the life process itself, in all its manifestations, on all levels. Failing to make the connections, we fall into the trap of the controllers' propaganda which claims that losing nature is desirable because her offspring is less viable, less healthy, less efficient than the reconstructed products.

Some feminists and many well-meaning women have latched on to artificial procreation as a means of achieving equality between the sexes and eliminating the emotional traumas arising from the power structure of the nuclear family. Thus, they urge women to take control of the reproductive technologies as weapons in the fight for our liberation from patriarchal rule.[18] To regain control of our sexuality – which includes our procreative capacity – is undoubtedly the key to our autonomy. But, however seductive the prospect of non-womb procreation may seem to some, it only frees women to become better men, that is, to join the dehumanising work force removed from the realities of our bodies and unencumbered by the interruptions and effects of negative body images and fears associated with pregnancy.

Like all other patriarchal institutions, non-womb procreation comes from the hands of men and will remain in their hands, no matter how many women choose to collaborate with it, directly as in the case of female scientists and technicians or indirectly, as in the case of women consumers. Artificial procreation leads to artificial life. It is a warped concept, even as wars and the manufacture of toxic substances are warped. Like these, it is founded on necrophilia since it requires the 'sacrifice' of animal life as well as of the human experimental subjects conned into 'participation'. Moreover, because the technology comes between women and our bodies, it further severs women from our connections with nature and as such is destructive of our integrity.

Eugenics

> The universe is sacred.
> You cannot improve it.
> If you try to change it, you will ruin it.
> If you try to hold it, you will lose it.
>
> Lao Tsu, *Tao Te Ching*

Super products

We take for granted roses and cows, peas and chickens, wheat and sheep, dogs, lettuce, and all that feeds us or that we choose to bring into our gardens and houses. All are 'improvements' of their respective original species. All are products of selective breeding, crosses and/or genetic manipulation. The first agriculturalists practised eugenics by selecting and planting successively larger seeds. The size of barley and maize increased gradually. Their integrity being untouched, they retained their fertility and nutritional value.

Ever since G.J. Mendel introduced the element of predictability into hereditary genetics while working on the hybridisation of peas, it has become possible to produce high-yield (socially productive) crops of the utmost uniformity. As man's will to control intensified with his successes, so did his objectification of plant (and animal) life. Modern eugenics shifts the motivation behind selection from producing nourishing, tasteful food, to manufacturing food for profit.

In a similar effort to improve their livestock and increase their profits, husbands* have practised artificial inovulation and insemination

---

* I use 'husband' here and throughout in its not-so-archaic sense of 'manager of a household' which includes wife, children, relatives, servants and animals. In bed and barn, husbands have exerted control over procreation for centuries.

for decades. 'High-grade' female animals are injected with chemicals to release a surplus of eggs from the ovaries – for example, cows can be induced to release forty or more eggs in a single cycle. The eggs are 'recovered' from the uterus of the 'high-grade' female, either frozen or stored in the oviduct of a living 'lower' animal (rabbits), and reimplanted in the uterus of a healthy but 'lesser-grade' female. In the converse of this procedure, the semen of an 'outstanding male' is collected, sometimes frozen for later use, then inserted in the womb of a 'high-grade' female at the right time in her cycle for conception. These techniques enable husbands to breed large quantities of top quality livestock, racing horses, show dogs, etc. around the globe.

A prize cow can be induced to ovulate every two months. A prize bull can sire more than 50,000 offspring in a year. He is kept in a stall and barely allowed to move. The concern is obviously not to ensure the preservation of life. Cows and bulls know how to do that on their own. The concern is to produce 'the best' offspring that will command the highest price in the marketplace. 'The best' is defined as 'basic structural correctness, stature, size, plus femininity in the females. You don't want them looking like steers.'[19] (No, *we* would not!) 'The best' is also defined by efficiency and ease of handling. Thus, during the past twenty years, husbands have paid increasing attention to the milking rate of cows as well as to the best size and placement of teats for machine milking. Udder development and teats are measured together with the milk record of cows in order to obtain a basis for gene selection and help produce 'better' cows.

Likewise, the spirit of free enterprise permeates efforts in human eugenics. There is talk of 'embryo supermarkets', where ready-to-thaw embryos with specified characteristics would be implanted and gestate in artificial wombs 'to eliminate mothers' contamination',[20] and to offer quality products instead.[21] Misogyny, violence, and the lust to control are evident everywhere. 'We shoot for good quality work.' We 'handle eggs'. We manipulate sperm (called 'ballistic missiles') 'to attack the egg' so that it will produce Supermen. And Super*men* it will mostly be, for according to one report, the ideal ratio of female to male ranges from 20–80 to 30–70.[22] Human eugenics and the accompanying reproductive technologies offer modern, sophisticated state-of-the-art methods of gynocide. Cruder efforts at this are common worldwide. India and China practise female infanticide as a matter of course, either through abortion of the foetus after amniocentesis or immediately after birth by 'drowning, suffocation, poisoning and desertion of baby girls'. According to Michael Weisskopf, in China 'official population statistics indicate a loss of more than 230,000 baby girls in 1981, a casualty list that is said to have grown dramatically in more recent years as the Communist government tightened its nationwide policy limiting Chinese couples to one child. Authorities have refused to reveal sex ratios after 1981.' He further reports the explanation of the women of Anhui Province as to why they had so many children. 'Why do we keep having babies and risking our health? Because there is no place in this world for those without sons. Even if it means death, we will keep trying for a son so that we may hold our heads high.'[23] Similarly, throughout Hispanic countries a man is not considered manly unless he produces a son. To avoid the consequences of the slurs on the father's personality if she 'fails', the woman is pressured to keep on trying for a boy, regardless of her health and ability to care for the children.

Eugenics is for everyone, like a two-car garage, a swimming pool in the backyard, a colour television and a couple of bright, quality kids at home. Robert K. Graham, an optometrist who made a fortune on his invention of plastic contact lenses, wants a bright race. He collects the sperm of old men, all Nobel prize recipients, at the 'Graham Repository for Germinal Choice' on his farm in Escondido, California. 'He does not provide valuable sperm to just any interested or smart [married] female; he thinks that only one of every fifty women is qualified to bear the children of Nobelists.'[24] To date, a number of such children have been born. 'These kids will sail through schools', Graham says. 'We are indicating how good human beings can have it.'[25] Upwards of 750 women applied for the 'privilege' of being artificially inseminated and birthing 'these kids'. 'These kids' are little better than clones intended to replicate white male genius, sailing through schools to contribute more to social 'improvement': more uniformity, more destruction of integrity, more diminishing of life.

What is hidden in Escondido ('escondido' is Spanish for 'hidden') and elsewhere is an inability to deal with diversity, as well as with real social problems such as sexism, racism, poverty in a land of plenty, environmental and stress-related abnormalities and diseases. It is faster and more efficient to select sperm donors of presumed intelligence and desirable ethnicity ('no fat men, no long ears, no hook noses') than it is to confront one's own fears or to eliminate one's prejudices.

As with plants and animals, human genes, it seems, can be divided into flowers and weeds, pets and pests. Directly linked to the active selection of 'high-quality' sperm or eggs to ensure a 'top-notch' human gene pool, is the active elimination of undesirable genes from the pool by the 'self-elected' sterilisation of the unfit. In the early 1900s, Margaret Sanger, well known for her activism for birth control and less remembered for her stand on eugenics, advocated government-sponsored sterilisation as 'the solution' to the problem of fertility among the 'unfit'.[26]

> It is a curious but neglected fact that the very types which in all kindness should be obliterated from the human stock, have been permitted to reproduce themselves and to perpetuate their group, succored by the policy of indiscriminate charity of warm hearts uncontrolled by cool heads. . . .
> There is only one reply to a request for a higher birth rate among the intelligent and that is to ask government to first take the burden of the insane and feebleminded from your back. . . . Sterilization is the solution.[27]

In an updated version of this suggestion, Nobel prize winner William Shockley proposed 'voluntary' sterilisation programmes for welfare recipients whereby a volunteer would be paid $1,000 for every I.Q. point s(he) scored below the mean (100) if s(he) consented to sterilisation.[28] Needless to say, welfare recipients are for the most part female, black, unschooled and very poor.[29]

In a speciesist, sexist, racist, and classist society, it takes little sophistication to realise along what uniform lines the human race is being husbanded eugenically. It is also not surprising to find in the ranks of the husbands instances of the very human characteristics destined for elimination – identification with the oppressor, self-hatred, self-deception.[30] Animals, at least, are innocent of such complicity.

Cloning

The engineering of the human species is a replay of Genesis in which man projected his need for mirrors upon his God by inventing a God who created man in his image. Nothing fulfils this need better than the clone (from Greek, *klōn*, 'twig'), the asexual reproduction of an individual from embryonic cells. The mirror-function of the clone replaces the traditional role of woman as provider of what Virginia

Woolf called man's 'looking-glass vision', that is, the mirror in which he sees himself as twice his natural size before going to work every morning. She saw clearly that 'mirrors are essential to all violent and heroic action', the looking-glass vision being the source of man's power: 'take it away and man may die, like the drug fiend deprived of his cocaine'.[31]

The need for mirrors is strongest during repressive regimes. Woolf cites the Czars and Kaisers, Hitler and Mussolini, as official reinforcers of woman's inferiority through measures and pronouncements that put her 'in her place', which is against the wall. Were Woolf alive today, she would undoubtedly have added the vast international conglomerates in control of production and reproduction, of which today's world 'leaders' are but sorry puppets.

Though the human application of cloning is at this point the least refined of all the reproductive technologies, it is the one that promises the most in terms of providing both a sense of omnipotence and a hall of mirrors. By 'creating' man in his image, the scientist becomes God. By surrounding himself with mirrors which he controls, he is able to carry on a love affair with his reflections.

Whether for or against human cloning, scientists agree that its realisation lies in the near future. As long ago as 1972 embryologist Leon Kass predicted that:

> Given the rate at which the other technical obstacles have fallen, and given the increasing number of competent people entering the field of experimental embryology, it is reasonable to expect the birth of the first cloned mammal sometime in the next few years. This will almost certainly be followed by a rush to develop cloning for other animals, especially livestock. . . . With the human embryo culture and implantation technologies being perfected in parallel, the step to the first clonal man [*sic*] might require only a few additional years.[32]

Mammal cloning was in fact first reported in 1981.[33] Kass does not favour human cloning. Biochemist Joshua Lederberg does. In *Who Should Play God?*, Howard and Rifkin discuss Lederberg's position.

> [Lederberg] hopes that 'we can clear up many uncertainties about the interplay of heredity and environment; and students of human nature will not want to waste such opportunities.' At the very least, he says, we could enjoy 'being able to observe the experiment of discovering whether a second

Einstein would outdo the first one.' . . . Lederberg sees no reason why an entire clone can't be grown and kept in storage against the day you have a medical problem – 'free exchange of organ transplants with no concern for graft rejection.'[34]

The search for omnipotence is at the core of the eugenicist's research. The human clone not only will be genetically controlled but its every thought and action will be scrutinised, monitored, tested, compared; its body will be 'held in storage' (how? where?). The clone provides the ultimate in an experimental subject/object because it is literally an objectified self.

According to French biologist Jean Rostand, discovering how to 'cause life to be born for the second time' would have no military, commercial or industrial repercussions.[35] It would simply 'exalt man'. In this context of male exaltation, it is important to remind ourselves that women have always known how to bring about life, and a few have even reproduced parthenogenetically, meaning the egg spontaneously divides without assistance from the sperm, develops and results in the birth of a girl child.[36] Yet woman's procreative power has been caricatured as tyrannical, devalued as defective and 'contaminated', sadistically exploited ('Keep her barefoot and pregnant'), punished ('Thus God chastised Eve: I will multiply your pains in childbearing. You shall give birth to your children in pain', Genesis 3:16), and idealised as a limitless, gratuitous source of nurturance and comfort available to men.

A requisite for exalting man is the debasing of life. Rostand defines life as a mere arrangement of matter, a problem of form and structure. Life as such does not exist other than as a philosophical concept. It is a property of matter, of a particular life form, an architectural design such as a potato, a beetle, an octopus, a human being. Therefore, 'the problem of the artificial creation of life . . . does not, or at any rate should not, stir up any passions; the synthesis of a living particle cannot prove or disprove any philosophical doctrine.

Rostand's notes and journals are full of the cynicism one might expect from a man who feels misunderstood because ahead of his time. He dismisses disagreement as stupid hostility and regressivism. He meets it with insults directed at the enemies of science, among whom are women. 'Truths are like women,' he writes. 'They would not stir up any passion if one could foresee what becomes of them in the course of time.' 'When I feel too alienated from the times I live in, the only thing to do is return to my frogs,' because, he informs us, 'biologists go, frogs remain'.[37] Rostand tortured many frogs in his experiments – those frogs did not remain. To someone who holds such an impoverished view of life in which truths and women go stale and experimenting on frogs is the content of life ('science or silence'), to someone who cannot tolerate disagreement and appreciate diversity, a clone is the perfect answer to 'the problem of life'.

Subhumans/monsters

The products of technological and experimental research – human–animal hybrids, human–computer and human–animal–computer combinations – have been variously designated chimeras, subhumans, parahumans, humanoids, etc. When these products deviate from the bio-engineers' designs, they are called 'monsters'. Gross abnormalities resulting from their mistakes are spoken of as 'teratogenic effects' (from Greek, *teras*, monster), while their successes are named 'chimeras', after a monster of Greek mythology. In the latter case, the notions of monster and abnormalities are removed as though by a process of mental ablation. The word 'chimera', distanced from its true meaning, allows the scientists to perceive their 'creations' as normal. One meaning of 'normal' is that which is statistically prevalent. Thus, it is more accurate to speak of their fabrications as hideously abnormal since they deviate from the statistically prevalent natural designs.

The very fact that subhumans and monsters (chimeras) are equated, however mindlessly, in the language of those engaged in human reproductive research points to the need for reviewing the older meaning of 'monster'. If nothing else, it will show that in concept, design, and function, monsters have nothing in common with their scientific counterparts. Imagination created far more complex combinations than science, without torturing animals and humans in the process.

We no longer remember our original relationship with monsters. It goes back far into prehistory and much has happened since to vitiate our understanding of them. Many human emotions and basic moral attitudes went into the concept of monster. Monsters were conceived as unifying forces: self with self, self with community, community with nature. In every culture, monsters have been imagined as composites made up of recognisable parts but as an entity belonging to no particular species, defying logic and mocking reason. Monsters were the known and the unknown, at once friendly and frightening, revered and dreaded, in short, awesome.

In *Daughters of Copper Woman*, Anne Cameron gives us the Nootka story of the monster Sisiutl – a story which offers better insight into the function of monsters than any of the Greek equivalents with which we are more familiar. The image and function of Sisiutl are closer to the original sense of 'monster' because his story has been preserved within the *living* memory (oral tradition) of the people who imagined him. Thus, the tale of Sisiutl, verbally transmitted from generation to generation, has been far less radically subjected to the iconoclastic waves of patriarchal conquerors than solely written traditions.

> Sisiutl, the fearsome monster of the sea. Sisiutl who sees from front and back. Sisiutl the soul searcher. . . . When you see Sisiutl you must stand and face him. Face the horror. Face the fear. If you break faith with what you Know, if you try to flee, Sisiutl will blow with both mouths at once and you will begin to spin . . . alone, and lonely, and lost forever.[38]

Sisiutl is the representation of the active search for truth contained in the emotion of fear itself. He hounds those who flee from themselves. He blesses those who stand firm and own their fears. Sisiutl obsesses those who deny the realities of their human condition.

Predictably, it is to the misogynistic rendering of the Greek myths that scientists in this culture have turned for most of their naming. The Chimera was a fire-breathing goat with a lion's head and a serpent's body who, together with her sisters, the Hydra and the Sphinx, was a symbol of the Great Goddess in Greece and throughout the Middle East.[39] It is important to note that she was not considered abnormal, ugly, or mean. These associations appeared only in the patriarchal reworkings of the older myths where they are referred to as monsters of terrifying impact. In the older myths they were simply given a personal name (Medusa, Gorgon, Hydra, Chimera, etc.) and functioned much as Sisiutl did, as a way of connecting with the unknown.

Websters' New Collegiate Dictionary defines chimera as a scientific term, 'an individual, organ, or part consisting of tissues of diverse genetic constitution'. Grafts, transplants, genetic surgery, embryo manipulation, brain implants, and whatever else results in cross-species mutants and/or genetically diverse organisms and/or computerised biological material (cyborgs)[40] are chimeras/monsters. We can see that the biological chimera bears no conceptual resemblance to its namesake as is commonly believed in the scientific community. Far from having a unifying function, the biological chimera further fragments and alienates because the organism is an assembly of spare parts, like a Kitchen-Aid processor capable of taking assorted attachments to perform a variety of specific tasks.

Spare parts are needed to develop subhumans. Researcher Robert White of Case Western Reserve University and the Cleveland Metropolitan General Hospital is a head hunter specialising in head transplants. If 'head transplant' sounds too gruesome, we can minimise the effect by using the Greek word for head, *cephalon*, as he suggests (see page 59). Besides having some success in preserving the living brains of dogs and monkeys, he has transferred the decapitated heads of rats and monkeys on to the bodies of other decapitated rats and monkeys.[41] Until such time as techniques to connect the spinal cord to the head are perfected, White's transplanted heads are literally attached to bodies without feeling. White has also met with Russian experimenters involved in linking the heads of cats to 'artificial maintenance and sensing systems, creating biocybernetic guidance packages for implantation in air-to-air missiles'.[42] This type of research has obvious implications for such grandiosely destructive projects as 'Star Wars', although its ostensible purpose is related to both health and eugenics: health – to replace a defective human organ; eugenics – to fashion a race of superior products (hybrids).

However, research in head transplants and regeneration of the nerve tissue in severed spinal cords is too heavily subsidised by various federal agencies and international governments for it to be concerned with human 'wellbeing'. It suggests not only military use but government interest in absolute control of individual destinies. For this reason, statements such as White's, 'we can transplant heads of humans with hope [*sic*] of achieving reasonably normal people'[43] stand out as sheer hypocrisy and nonsense. We are shocked by the idea of a head transplant, not because it is qualitatively different from any other animal or human transplant, but because 'reasonably normal people' are singularly vain about the housing of their brains – the brain, of course, being the seat of our perception of the sensory world, of learning, of thinking, of memory, of moving and being moved, of consciousness and ultimately of the self. Of course there is more to it than vanity. The fabrication of chimeras to be herded together on 'farms' against the day a doctor finds a patient he can manipulate into wanting a replacement of an impaired organ is a way of warding off death, if only for a short (and very likely, miserable) time. Once all failing parts of a body are replaced, the *individual* has disappeared yet is 'immortal' by virtue of the fact that clinical death has been postponed.

The cost of postponing death is enormous, not only in financial terms – organ transplants cost a fortune – but more importantly in animal and human terms. For the animals, it is always certain death. For the post-operative patient, it means specialised technical assistance in order to be kept alive. If life is understood as the mere functioning of one's internal systems and one accepts the subsequent dependence on drugs, doctors, and family to keep further deterioration and side-effects in check, the most one can expect from these medical 'advances' is a short extension of a passive non-life, which amounts to the same thing as a non-death, that is, neither here nor there.

It is assumed that more research on animal and human experimental subjects will eventually lead to the refinement of today's organ transplant techniques through a more thorough understanding of the graft rejection problem. It is immaterial that today's techniques may work a little better than those of a decade ago and therefore might work better yet in the future.[44] The point is that even smooth transfer of organs from a 'donor' to the human host, and less dependence on continued medical aid, do not justify organ banks in the form of animals, humans,* or subhumans. The human species (and a selective portion at that) should not proliferate and prolong its life-span at the expense

---

* See discussion of Lederberg's proposed use of clones to provide an individual with replacement parts of identical genetic composition, above, p.120.

animal and human subjects. For there is no doubt that the people on whom this technology is tried and perfected are like the experimental animals, just so many test cases that could lead to the total surrender of our humanity.

A case in point, where nature's designs/creations, humanity, and indeed, life itself are mocked, is the 'mothering man' to be produced with organ transplants, reproductive technologies and hormonal injections. Joseph Fletcher describes the feasibility of such a chimera in *The Ethics of Genetic Control*:

> a uterus can be implanted in a human male's body – his abdomen has spaces – and gestation started by artificial fertilization and egg transfer. Hypogonadism could be used to stimulate milk from man's rudimentary breasts – men too have mammary glands. If surgery could not construct a cervical canal the delivery could be affected by Caesarian section and the male transsexualized mother could nurse his own baby.[45]

Indeed! Can there be any clearer, more extreme statement of male womb envy and desire to appropriate female power by eliminating woman and nature?

Another way of trying to 'improve' the species is by calling upon cybernetics to eliminate not only physical human shortcomings but emotional ones as well. This is accomplished by manufacturing electronic chimeras – human–computer (and animal–computer) conglomerates called cyborgs (see page 86). These may be humanoid robots or computerised humans and animals in any feasible combination, since the envisaged cyborg is the product of biochemical, physiological and electronic manipulation.

Thus, biocybernetics and genetic engineering both play a part in the electronic chimera, a structure capable of what scientists in these fields call 'participant evolution' – a term that refers to man's replacement of hereditary genetics with the engineers' notion of a better adapted, healthier, more intelligent restructured 'Man'. In this way, man 'participates' in his own evolution away from biological destiny toward computerised perfection.

All these eugenic efforts show clearly the patriarch's inability to live life, to take joy (en-joy) and hardship in his stride. He construes life as a *struggle* for survival, as a *problem* to be solved, instead of as an experience to be lived. Because he cannot live life, he cannot let live. The whole idea behind restructuring the species lies in an attempt to compensate for this deadness by overpowering life.

I see team upon team of eugenicists converging on laboratory animals and electronic machinery like vultures on a carcass exposed in the desert. I see billions of government monies taken from people around the world, earmarked for military, space, and domestic research, being spent on perfecting a total man–machine 'partnership'.[46] I read everywhere that all this is happening for our safety, our wellbeing, our convenience (robots to vacuum our carpets and clean our toilets, for instance), our mental and physical health, our craving for adventure. I see that people are standing in line for organ transplants, the new reproductive technologies, biofeedback, robots, computers, videogames, all of which are but a short step away from the chimera, subhuman, parahuman, cyborg. And as we wait in those lines, we would do well to contemplate the fact that we are not just what we eat but also what we connect with.

The experimental nursery

> [The behaviorist] brings the newborn individual *into his experimental nursery* and begins to set problems. (Watson's emphasis)
>
> John Watson, *Behaviorism*

Behind man's scientific 'divine intervention' lies an enfeebled imagination crippled by fear and envy, in particular of woman's reproductive powers. Having interfered with the biological processes of pregnancy and birthing, man is left with the bonding of mother and infant, a phenomenon that exacerbates his sense of impotence and alienation from nature and life. However, if he can prove that such a bond is replaceable, or better still, capable of being dispensed with altogether, he will have eliminated the last vestige of any need for a connection to the world of nature as symbolised/embodied in woman and most dramatically in the image and reality of mother.

The invisible hand that runs through the culture and separates mother from child is nowhere more blatant than in the laboratory. In a series of deprivation studies designed to produce pathology in animals, Harry and Margaret Harlow separated infant monkeys from their mothers a few hours after birth and raised them in isolation, sometimes for as long as two years. They chose the monkey because it was 'morally and physically impossible' to conduct this investigation with human subjects.[47]

Like humans, however, monkeys need a long developmental period during which the young are intimately attached to their mothers. By depriving them of this basic need, the Harlows 'succeeded' in producing abnormalities they admit are seldom seen in animals born in the wild but are common in children reared in orphanages as well as in withdrawn adolescents and adults confined in mental hospitals.

> [The monkeys] sit in their cages and stare fixedly into space, circle their cages in a repetitive stereotyped manner and clasp their heads in their hands or arms and rock for long periods of time. They often develop compulsive habits, such as pinching precisely the same patch of skin on the chest between the same fingers hundreds of times a day; occasionally such behavior may become punitive and the animal may chew and tear at its body until it bleeds. Often the approach of a human being becomes the stimulus to self-aggression.[48]

Whether from want of more monkeys or from a morbid interest in their sexual behaviour, these experimental pioneers attempted to 'bring about matings, by pairing animals during the female's oestrus' and found that the motherless infants, who in their youth had been unresponsive to other monkeys and had displayed no heterosexual interest, 'sometimes fought so viciously that they had to be parted',[49] when confronted with a mate. To remedy what the Harlows called this 'aberration' – the monkeys', of course – they devised an 'aberrant' apparatus dubbed 'the rape rack'. Thus, they forced the female monkeys into pregnancy and the 'problem' the Harlows manufactured in one generation could be traced to the next. The motherless females who were induced' to conceive rejected their infants at birth.

> [In some cases they] were brutal or lethal. One of their favorite tricks was to crush the infant's skull with their teeth. But the really sickening behavior pattern was that of smashing the infant's face to the floor, then rubbing it back and forth.[50]

A mother driven to reject and kill her offspring is a tragic figure. Her behaviour is neither abnormal nor sickening. Rather, it is the behaviour of the Harlows – who deliberately engineered the circumstances which drove her to it – which is abnormal and sickening.[51] Moreover, pregnancy and birthing in themselves are not necessarily connected to mothering. These monkeys were brutally deprived of mothering, both as infants and as mothers themselves.

Other Harlow experiments led to 'the discovery of the unimportant or non-existent role of the breast and act of nursing'.[52] Swinging plastic bottles wrapped in furry cloth and most of all, infant–infant interaction can replace mother. 'It seems possible – even likely – that the mother affectional system is dispensable, whereas the infant-infant system is the *sine qua non* for later adjustment in all spheres of monkey life.'[53] It does not matter how one interprets these experiments. I am not impressed in the least that they led to the formulation of a theory of motherhood used as a counterbalance to Freud's: Freud condemned women to motherhood ('anatomy is destiny') and the Harlows showed that mothering is incidental to them, an aggregate of learned behaviours determined by early experience. One is as false as the other. We live in a world in which *all* reality, including woman's, is male-defined. Therefore, these men's theories of what is and what is not involved in mothering have no basis in a woman's truth, but in pathology: the pathology of the experiment as well as rank misogyny.

The Harlows and their team were not exceptional in their efforts to destroy the significance and the reality of mothering. José Delgado also is fascinated by the mother–infant bond. He found a faster way to break and restore it at will with ESB (electrical stimulation of the brain).

> If the [mother rhesus monkey and her infant] are forcibly separated, the mother becomes very disturbed and expresses her anxiety by prowling about restlessly, threatening observers, and calling to her baby with a special cooing sound. It is promptly reciprocated by the little one, who is also extremely anxious to return to the protective maternal embrace. This strong bond can be inhibited by ESB.[54]

> Maternal affection was expressed as usual without being handicapped by the presence of electrodes implanted [in the mother. With the application of brain stimulation to a certain area of her brain] an aggressive attitude was evoked with rapid circling around the cage and self-biting of the hand, leg, or flank. In the next 8-10 minutes, [the mother] completely lost interest in her baby, ignoring his tender calls and rejecting his attempts to approach her. [The baby] looked rather disoriented and sought refuge and

warmth with the other mother. About 10 minutes after ESB [the mother of the infant accepted the baby in her arms]. This experiment was repeated several times on different days with similar disruptive results for the mother/infant relationship.[55]

Clearly, mothers have good cause to mistrust fathers' experimental excursions into the nursery. ESB inhibition of the mother–infant bond, the non-existent role of the breast and the act of nursing, as well as the expendability of mother's 'affectional system' are findings that diminish woman, victimise and/or eliminate mothers, and damage the child.

The scientists' contentions that the breast and the act of nursing are not essential to the child fit quite nicely into the profit columns of the manufacturers of infant formula, their profits being made at the expense of the mother–infant bond, and often, in 'developing' countries, at the expense of the child's life.

> Evidence from developing countries indicates that infants breast-fed less than six months, or not at all, have a mortality rate 5–10 times higher in the second six months of life than those breast-fed six months or more.[56]
>
> The studies are conclusive. Failure to breast-feed in rural developing communities is tantamount to a death sentence.[57]

Mothers, of course, are blamed for the high infant mortality because they misuse father's gift. Ignorantly, they wash the bottles in contaminated water, thus infecting their infants, and/or they water down the formula to make it last longer (a day's supply of formula can cost half a day's wages).

The 'need' for infant formula among mothers in 'developing' countries is linked to malnutrition in the mothers who no longer have adequate milk to nourish their infants; to the drying up of the woman's milk supply under the stress of city slum dwelling – a relocation brought about by the economic exploitation of 'developing' countries; to the absence of the mother from the home as a result of needed outside work. All this is the result of economic imperialism, a kind of exponential exploitation that spirals in ever-widening circles toward man's total control of life. Meanwhile, wherever woman is held in low esteem, anything that further diminishes her role will be readily adopted.

*

The ideological framework for the modern obsession with reproductive technologies, eugenics and maternal–infant bonding lies in androcentric myths. These myths reflect a profound hostility toward and resentment of the female body as well as a compulsive desire to appropriate its generative functions. The archetypal father begets life by destroying female presence and confiscating her magic, that is, her creative potency. Thus, pleased with himself for having slain and dismembered the Great Mother, Ti'âmat, the Babylonian god Marduk ponders 'the ingenious things' he can do with her body. He fashions the universe from her mutilated parts, deriving his power from her 'tablet of destinies' (her magic) which he has stolen.

The Hebrew god, Jahweh, is the male principle detached from nature and the realities of the senses. He is pure intellect. Severed from the life-cycle, his divine potency is a function of will. As in the Babylonian myth, bringing forth life for this god is not perceived as a process but as an act, a performance, a command and conquest over nature and woman. And in this idealised version, female presence is completely eliminated, since all of creation is wrought from the void.

In the Christian tradition, God the father is disembodied but the son becomes mysteriously incarnate through the artificial insemination of Mary by the holy ghost. As for the Greek mythologies, Zeus has a fondness for removing 'embryos' from their mothers' wombs, and implanting them in unlikely parts, carrying them and giving birth by himself – Athena from his forehead and Dionysus from his thigh. In classical Greece, Apollo – the reasonable god – wins the struggle over mother-right with the argument that all mothers are mere surrogates who mechanically and incidentally carry the male seed to fruition. 'The mother is no parent to that which is called her child, but only nurse of the new-planted seed that grows. The parent is he who mounts. A stranger she preserves a stranger's seed, if no god interfere.'[58] In these versions of life with father, man represents himself as cut off from his senses, 'a cripple in a cave', [59] attempting to surpass the female in her creativeness while lacking true creativity himself. He 'resolves' this inherent paradox through an intellectual swindle whereby the female is willed away and creation is redefined in his own terms.

The fathers have tried through their myths and through their science to disrupt what women know in our bodies and from our experiences. Yet, as expressed in the Nootka story of 'The Women's

Society', they have not and will not vanquish our wisdom.

> The priests thought they had destroyed the matriarchy. They saw fighting
> and drunkenness where once there was love and respect . . . They saw
> girls who should have been clan mothers become prostitutes in the cities
> the invaders built.

> A few women saved and protected the wisdom of the matriarchy, even at
> the risk of their lives. . . . Much was lost. Much will never be regained.
> We have only the shredded fragments . . . of learning. But torn as it is,
> fragmented as it is, it is still better than the ideas the invader brought with
> him.[60]

Notes

1. 'Children' is a misnomer in this case since Leah and Rachel and their
   surrogates are recorded as birthing nine sons and only one daughter,
   Dinah, who is casually mentioned and clearly incidental to the story. All
   quotes from the story of Leah and Rachel are taken from *The Jerusalem
   Bible, Reader's Edition* (Garden City, New York: Doubleday, 1968).
2. Claudia Wallis, 'The New Origins of Life', *Time* (10 September 1984),
   pp.46, 50.
3. For a discussion of the role of television in the elimination of inherent
   meaning see Jerry Mander, *Four Arguments for the Elimination of
   Television* (New York: William Morrow, 1978; Brighton: Harvester
   Press, 1980), pp.285–9.
4. Ted Howard and Jeremy Rifkin used the analogy of the Trojan horse in
   reference to recombinant DNA chimeras. See *Who Should Play God?*
   (New York: Dell Publishing Company, 1978), p.32.
5. [ME.; AS. <*giefan* (see GIVE + -t; influenced by the cognate ON. *gipt*,
   gift, what is given; akin to G. *gist*, poison)] *Websters' New World
   Dictionary of the American Language* (Cleveland, Ohio: The World
   Publishing Company, 1966).
6. Gena Corea, *The Mother Machine: Reproductive Technologies from
   Artificial Insemination to Artificial Wombs* (New York: Harper & Row,
   1985; London: The Women's Press, 1988), p.206.
7. ibid., pp.166–85.
8. As Mary Daly has pointed out, it is essential that the promoters of
   gynocide (read here: infertility) keep their secret invisible to everyone,
   especially to themselves through the promotion of the opposite/reversals
   (read here: fertility). *Gyn/Ecology: The Metaethics of Radical Feminism*
   (Boston: Beacon Press, 1978; London: The Women's Press, 1979),
   pp.90–1.

9. Ann Crittenden, 'More and more conglomerate links in US food chain', *The New York Times* (1 February 1981), p.E-3.

10. The siabon, the sterile hybrid offspring of a female siamang and a male gibbon housed together in Atlanta's Grant Park Zoo, is a case in point. With 'no reproductive future' in store for her, the siabon none the less '"lends some credence" the scientists say, to the possibility of creating human-ape hybrids, although they don't recommend it'. See 'Old evolutionary doctrines jolted by a hybrid ape', *The New York Times* (29 July 1979), and Stephen Jay Gould, 'The siabon: interesting but probably not fruitful', *The New York Times* (5 August 1979).

11. Claudia Wallis, 'The saddest epidemic', *Time* (10 September 1984), p.50.

12. Jamey L. Judge and Joyce J. Contrucci, 'The double standard, sexual permissiveness, and sexual aggression in heterosexual dating couples', unpublished paper, 1981.

13. Michael Castleman, 'Toxics and male infertility', *Sierra*, 70 (2) (March/April 1985), p.52.

14. ibid., p.49.

15. ibid., p.52.

16. Perri Klass, 'Bearing a child in medical school', *The New York Times Magazine* (11 November 1984), p.122.

17. Quoted ibid., p.123.

18. See Shulamith Firestone, *The Dialectic of Sex: The Case for Feminist Revolution* (New York: Bantam Books, 1971; London: The Women's Press, 1979), pp.238-9, and Nancy Breeze, 'Who's going to rock the petri dish?', *Trivia* (Spring 1984), pp.43-8.

19. Bart Barnes, 'Ranch uses sophisticated cattle breeding system', *Los Angeles Times* (5 August 1979), p.10.

20. Big-time laboratory animal breeder, Henry Foster had the same idea and the same spirit of free enterprise when he developed and marketed the specific pathogen-free animal. See Chapter 3, pp.73-4.

21. Associated Press report aired on station WEEI, Boston, Massachusetts, 25 October 1978.

22. Jay McMullen (producer/reporter), 'CBS Reports: The Baby Makers', aired on Channel 7, WNEV-TV, Boston, Massachusetts, 30 October 1979.

23. Michael Weisskopf, 'Killing daughters', *Newsday*, 13 February 1985.

24. Lori B. Andrews, 'Inside the genius farm', *Parents Magazine* (October 1980), p.82.

25. Quoted in Otto Friedrich, 'A legal, moral, social nightmare', *Time* (10 September 1984), p.56. In the field of human eugenics there also seems to be no concern with undoing gender stereotypes. Marilyn Monroe and Raquel Welch, with a handful of male geniuses – Beethoven, Kant and Einstein – are the names most quoted as examples of 'the best' human

selections.

26. Howard and Rifkin, *Who Should Play God?* p.57.

27. Margaret Sanger, 'Need for birth control in America', in Adolf Meyer (ed.), *Birth Control, Facts, and Responsibilities* (Baltimore: Williams & Williams, 1925), p.15.

28. Camille B. Wortman and Elizabeth F. Loftus, *Psychology*, 2nd edn (New York: Alfred A. Knopf, 1985), p.409.

29. Apparently the 'fit' are beating the 'unfit' in the race for self-elected sterilisation. According to a report issued by the National Center for Health Statistics, in 1982 sterilisation had become the most common form of birth control among married couples, a fact accounted for by the steady increase in *female* sterilisation from 7 per cent in 1965 to 26 per cent in 1982. See 'Studies show a dramatic rise in sterilization', *The New York Times* (9 December 1984), p.29.

30. Using brute force and 'persuasion' (brainwashing), Hitler aimed at a super Aryan race, sparing no atrocity in order to eliminate unwanted diversity. The self-hatred and self-deception manifested in his vision – Hitler himself was a far cry from his Aryan ideal, and so were his most cruel henchmen – should act as a warning signal in our evaluation of today's eugenicists.

31. Virginia Woolf, *A Room of One's Own* (New York: Harbinger Books, 1957; London: Panther, 1977, new edn), p.36.

32. Quoted in Vance Packard, *The People Shapers* (New York: Bantam Books Inc., 1977; London: Macdonald & Jane's, 1978), p.344.

33. The first cloned mammal was in fact reported on 4 January 1981. See Walter Sullivan, 'First cloning of mammals produces three mice', *The New York Times* (4 January 1981).

34. Howard and Rifkin, *Who Should Play God?*, p.123.

35. Jean Rostand, *Humanly Possible: A Biologist's Notes on the Future of Mankind*, translated by Lowell Bair (New York: Saturday Review Press, 1973), pp.153, 163. Fifteen years after Rostand expressed that opinion (1970) the 'life' technologies are a multibillion dollar business (1985).

36. David Rorvik *In His Image: The Cloning of a Man* (New York: Pocket Books, 1978), pp.97–80.

37. This and the two preceding quotes are my translations of Jean Rostand, *Inquiétudes d'un Biologiste* (Paris: Stock, 1967), pp.35, 115, and 53.

38. Anne Cameron, *Daughters of Copper Woman* (Vancouver: Press Gang Publishers, 1981; London: The Women's Press, 1984), p.45.

39. Robert Graves, *The Greek Myths*, vols. I and II (Baltimore, Maryland: Penguin Books Inc., 1957; London: Penguin Books, 1969), *passim*.

40. The word was coined in the 1960s by Manfred Clynes, inventor of the CAT (computerised axial tomography) computer and director of the Biocybernetic Laboratory, Rockland State Hospital.

41. Packard, *The People Shapers*, pp.409–13.
42. David Rorvik, *As Man Becomes Machine* (New York: Pocket Books, 1978; London: Souvenir Press, 1973), p.169.
43. Quoted in Packard, *The People Shapers*, p.414.
44. New anti-rejection drugs have improved the success rate of heart transplants since the pioneer work of Dr Christiaan N. Barnard in the late 1970s. In 1977 he implanted the heart of a female baboon into the chest of a 25-year-old Italian woman, in addition to her own ailing heart. The woman died several hours later. Again, he 'piggy-backed' a chimpanzee's heart into another patient who died several days later. In 1978 he reportedly abandoned the technique of using ape hearts in humans 'not because I'm so convinced I'm on the wrong track, but I got emotionally involved with the chimp'. (See Lawrence K. Altman, 'Learning from Baby Fae', *The New York Times*, 18 November 1984, p.1.)

   Dr Leonard Bailey and his colleagues who were responsible for the 1984 Baby Fae baboon-to-human heart transplant, were Seventh-Day Adventists who apparently developed no such feelings for their victims. Ironically to me, they took the delivery of health care as a 'life mission'. They believe that 'the body is the temple of God' to be well cared for, involving a vegetarian diet, exercise, and rest. (See Sandra Blakeslee, 'Doctor had been preparing for transplant over 7 years', *The New York Times*, 18 November 1984.) Clearly the body of the baboon is not regarded as a temple nor is it cared for in their 'life mission'.
45. Joseph Fletcher, *The Ethics of Genetic Control* (Garden City, New York: Anchor Books, 1974), p.45.
46. NASA is already on record as looking forward to this 'partnership', it being 'essential to the large-scale *exploitation* of space and the oceans' (emphasis mine). See Rorvik, *As Man Becomes Machine*, p.161.
47. Harry Harlow and Margaret Harlow, 'Social deprivation in monkeys', (November 1962) in Richard F. Thompson (Introductions), *Physiological Psychology: Readings from 'Scientific American'* (San Francisco: W.H. Freeman & Company, 1971), pp.315–23.
48. ibid., p.316.
49. ibid., p.317.
50. Quoted in Peter Singer, *Animal Liberation: A New Ethics for our Treatment of Animals* (New York: Avon Books, 1975; London: Jonathan Cape, 1976), p.49.
51. Twelve years into their deprivation studies and systematic isolation programmes, Harlow and Suomi found that complete social isolation of the infant from birth calls for a socially normal, chronologically younger 'therapist' monkey who can lead the depressed and withdrawn isolates step by step to displaying 'the full vigor and vivacity of social play'.

They are impressed when their paternal interventions into maternal care proceed to turn monkeys showing protest, despair, excessive clinging, maturational arrest into normally-behaving monkeys after play sessions with age-mate therapists. See Stephen J. Suomi, 'Factors affecting responses to social separation in rhesus monkeys', in George Serban and Arthur Kling (eds.), *Animal Models in Human Psychobiology* (New York: Plenum Press, 1976), p.23.

52. Harry Harlow, 'Love in infant monkeys', (June 1959) in Thompson (Introductions), *Physiological Psychology: Readings from 'Scientific American'*, p.84.
53. Harry Harlow and Margaret Harlow, 'Social deprivation in monkeys', p.316.
54. José M.R. Delgado, *Physical Control of the Mind: Toward a Psychocivilized Society* (New York: Harper & Row, 1969), p.168.
55. ibid., pp.168-9.
56. Halfdan Mahler, director general of the World Health Organization, quoted in Stephen Solomon, 'The controversy over infant formula', *The New York Times Magazine* (6 December 1981), p.102.
57. Dr Nevin Scrimshaw, director of the MIT-Harvard International Food and Nutrition Program, quoted in Solomon, 'The controversy over infant formula', p.104.
58. Aeschylus, 'The Eumenides', in *The Complete Greek Tragedies, vol. 1, Aeschylus*, eds. David Grene and Richard Lattimore (Chicago, Illinois: University of Chicago Press, 1959), p. 158, lines 657-61.
59. See Virginia Woolf, *Three Guineas* (New York: Harbinger Books, 1963; London: Hogarth Press, 1976, new edn), p.72. 'What remains of a human being who has lost sight, sound, and sense of proportion? Only a cripple in a cave.'
60. Cameron, *Daughters of Copper Woman*, pp.62-3.

5. Facing the future

As man proceeds toward his announced goal of the conquest of nature, he has written a depressing record of destruction, not only against the earth he inhabits but against the life that shares it with him.

Rachel Carson, *Silent Spring*

You have been having our rights so long, that you think, like a slave-holder, that you own us. I know that it is hard for one who has held the reins for so long to give up; it cuts like a knife. It will feel all the better when it closes up again.

Sojourner Truth, 'Keeping the Thing Going while Things Are Stirring

It is a land with neither night nor day,
 Nor heat nor cold, nor any wind nor rain,
 Nor hills nor valleys: but one even plain
stretches through long unbroken miles away . . .
 No beat of wings to stir the stagnant space:
 No pulse of life through all the loveless land
And loveless sea; no trace of days before . . .
No future hope, no fear for evermore.

Christina Rossetti, 'Cobwebs'

The Indian Way is a different way. It is a respectful
way. . . . Your 'civilization' has made all of us very
sick and has made our mother earth sick and out of
balance. Your kind of thinking and education has
brought the whole world to the brink of total disaster.

Carol Lee Sanchez, Native American
'Sex, class and race intersections:
visions of women of colour',
Sinister Wisdom, 22/23

Women and ecology

We are the rocks, we are soil, we are trees, rivers,
we are wind, we carry the birds, we are cows, mules,
we are horses, we are Solid elements . . . matter. *We*
are flesh, we breathe, we are her body: we speak.

Susan Griffin, *Woman and Nature*

The identity and destiny of woman and nature are merged. Accordingly, feminist values and principles directed towards ending the oppression of women are inextricably linked to ecological values and
principles directed towards ending the oppression of nature. These
values and principles are distilled from women's experiences everywhere and of all times. Their realisation for women and the earth is
predicated on women and men refusing to endorse the destructive
values that drive sexism, racism, classism, and speciesism. It is
ultimately the affirmation of our kinship with nature, of our common
life with her, which will prove the source of our mutual wellbeing.

Ecology is woman-based almost by definition. *Eco* means house,
logos means word, speech, thought. Thus ecology is the language of
the house. Defined more formally, ecology is the study of the interconnectedness between all organisms and their surroundings – the
house. As such, it requires a thorough knowledge and an intimate experience of the house.

Good women have kept good houses on the model of Mother
Nature for as long as there have been mothers. They have seen to it
that their children were fed, clothed, sheltered and safe. They have
kept the budget (eco/nomics) delicately balanced between extra-

vagance and thrift, often at incredible cost to themselves. Starvation and squalor have occurred only under extreme patriarchal control of the production of the land and children. Even then, as under less stringent degrees of oppression, many women have weathered abuse just as many creatures of the earth, air and water have survived man-made cataclysms, with resilience and regeneration. Like weeds and pests that have become immune to chemical poisoning, they have kept their wildness, that is, their strength and insubordination to outside control by maintaining their ties to each other.

Women's experience with oppression and abuse, as well as their experience of mothering, can make them more sensitive to the oppression and abuse of nature, as well as better situated to remedy it. Feminists in particular can enrich the base of ecology with their own theoretical analyses and intimate experience of the house. Love and anger drive feminists to achieve the goals of non-violence, reproductive freedom, creature rights for all, and rigorous house-cleaning. For women, this means an understanding and sweeping rejection of all behavioural debris that keeps us divided and makes us complicit in our oppression. It means rescuing our wildness and being proud of it. As it concerns nature, it means cleaning up the existing messes we have made through thoughtlessness and greed as well as taking off our shoes before entering the house, the ecosphere of our activities, as if we were entering a sanctuary, for the sheer joy and celebration of it.

In *Woman and Nature* (1977), Susan Griffin draws on this deep, life-sustaining interconnection between women and the earth. Her words, harsh and accurate when she addresses the facts of man's violence against nature, impassioned and grieving when she speaks of the experience of those facts, stir 'what is still wild in us', moving us along with her to a profound sense of loss and a vibrant reclamation of the earth, our sister/mother. She writes

> This earth is my sister; I love her daily grace, her silent daring, and how loved I am *how we admire this strength in each other, all that we have lost, all that we have suffered, all that we know: we are stunned by this beauty, and I do not forget; what she is to me, what I am to her.*[1]

In a different vein but with a great deal of feeling for the unintended victims of chemical insecticides, Rachel Carson began sending out her 'house message' over forty years ago, at a time that places her in the vanguard of the ecological movement. She is best remembered as a fighter against the use of DDT but she has also written a moving account of 'that great mother of life, the sea'. In *The Sea Around Us* (1951), she saw clearly that

> man, unhappily, has written one of his blackest records as a destroyer of the oceanic islands. He has seldom set foot on an island that he has not brought about disastrous changes. He has destroyed environments by cutting, clearing, and burning. . . . Upon species after species of island life, the black night of extinction has fallen.[2]

And again in *Silent Spring* (1962), she refers to the use of the insecticide DDT with words that ring sadly familiar to us, as the peddlers of 'better' substances (dioxin, EDB) continue to poison us.

> As man proceeds toward his announced goal of the conquest of nature, he has written a depressing record of destruction, directed not only against the earth he inhabits but against the life that shares it with him. . . . Under the philosophy that now seems to guide our destinies, nothing must get in the way of the man with the spray gun.[3]

The man with the (spray) gun is still very much alive. He is a man for whom the industry and practices of war carry over into the industry and practices of peace, the male counterpart of Mirabel Morgan's Total Woman, the man obsessed with Total Control.

In *Earth's Aura* (1977), Louise B. Young addresses man's greed and drive for power, although without the polemic spirit of Carson's *Silent Spring*. Like Carson, she believes that scientists do not know enough yet to tamper with natural forces and, like Carson, she combines impressive scientific knowledge with the awareness that we are embarked on a disastrous course. Her book generates an aura of its own, invoking a wholeness of vision and involvement with nature as a wonder-ful living organism deserving of our care. As she puts it:

> It would be useful to think of the planet earth surrounded by its halo of gases, as though it were a living organism – to sense its changing needs, to protect its flow of sunshine, bind its wounds, and treat it with the same loving gentleness we accord to a flower, or a child.[4]

Writing in the activist, ecological tradition of Rachel Carson,

Helen Caldicott shocked her readers into awareness with the appearance of her book *Nuclear Madness* (1978).[5] The threat to the wellbeing of all life posed by nuclear technologies is so grave and the necessity of thoroughly cleaning the house of its deadly by-products is so urgent, that Caldicott's work merits close attention.

Nuclear Madness is to the nuclear industry what *Silent Spring* was to the manufacturing and commercial use of DDT in the United States. Helen Caldicott, as Rachel Carson sixteen years earlier, received mixed criticism – on the one hand, applause for clear, eye-opening expositions of the facts; and on the other, attempts to discredit her work as alarmist, a one-sided and emotional distortion of the facts. The attacks came, respectively, from those heavily committed to nuclear technology and from those who had a vested interest in profitable agricultural programmes based on the use of the insecticide DDT. Both women were said to lack proper qualifications, as if being trained in one field (Caldicott is a physician; Carson was a marine biologist) precluded one's ability to do thorough research in another and to write intelligently about it. Both were blamed for not presenting both sides of the problem, as if one had to make a case in favour of destruction and death in order to make one in favour of life. Both were criticised for emotionalism because they wrote with feeling and a sense of compassion. Both were said to be alarmists because there is an either/or quality to their conclusions that is impossible to ignore. In the case of *Nuclear Madness*, either we act or we die of cancer; we act or we expose all life to gross genetic mutations; we act or – as the film *The Day After* also made dramatically clear – we blow up the earth and extinguish all life.

In *Nuclear Madness*, although the focus of the environmental crisis is on nuclear technology, there are some memorable no-nonsense questions and statements about human psychology which confront us with our fears and disarm us of our rationalisations. For example, concerning the human ability to deny reality, she asks:

> Is it not remarkable how we manage to live our lives in apparent normality, while, at every moment, human civilization and the existence of all forms of life on our planet are threatened with sudden annihilation? We seem to accept this situation calmly, as if it were to be expected. . . . But soothing our anxiety by ignoring the constant danger of annihilation will not lessen the danger.[6]

After illustrating some of the lies, cover-ups and ignorance of world leaders engaged in keeping the nuclear industry strong, Caldicott bluntly states that we cannot trust in their sanity and stability. This is a well-documented historical fact. The will-to-power carried to high political levels centres on military might and often leads to a belief in one's invulnerability. We all know the official line (national security through mutually assured destruction) used to rationalise the nuclear arms race and the installation of Pershing and Cruise missiles in countries which, if the decision were put to a referendum, would vote it out. What the proliferation of nuclear weapons guarantees for us all, however, is not security but the annihilation of life on this planet. Political leaders fuelling the arms race lose sight of another historical truth which Caldicott points out, namely that 'the drive for invulnerability leads to total vulnerability'.

Caldicott's experience with change has left her with a faith that, once informed, concerned citizens can turn into a political majority that would force a worldwide radical change in both government and industrial policies. This is indeed a great deal of faith, for in the political majority Caldicott includes the citizens of all those countries having nuclear capacity. She invokes the concept of the world citizen as she appeals for a worldwide, shoulder-to-shoulder sharing of responsibility for war and peace.

I reservedly share Caldicott's faith in the people's will 'to change society'. Judging from a growing consumerism, the plight of the earth, and the steady gap between the 'haves and the have-nots', most people seem bent on personal achievement and acquisition to the exclusion of social and ecological responsibility. They choose to ignore that their very lives are at stake and to cling to the notion that it is impossible to change society because it excuses them from involvement. However, I am encouraged by the swelling number of protesters, the activities of concerned scientists, and the example of those who, like the three physicists Caldicott mentions in her book, have had the courage to trust themselves, leave their positions, and stop contributing to the nuclear effort.

We live in a fragmented world full of divisive '-isms'. It does not help to disconnect them from one another. Like Athena, they sprang from the same god-head. Like Athena, they have been upheld by generations of women and men who have renounced their allegiance to the self as children of the Earth and Ocean Mother. If feminists and ecologists are to achieve real gains in eliminating oppression, it will be through a re-collection of our lost identity. It will involve a stark assessment of our silence, our tolerance of the intolerable, our apathy which is acquiescence. As Alice Walker suggests in *In Search of Our Mothers' Gardens*, the real cause for concern is our silence.

I think it is time to put ecology back into feminism, to feel as our own the plight of the earth and shout it. Otherwise feminism and ecology will continue to win only partial gains, buying time. Otherwise the supremacist mentality that rules the affairs of our planet will continue to run its destructive course and annihilate us all in the name of health, happiness and progress.

'Wooing' vs. 'loving'

Each of the women (authors/activists) discussed above expresses a deep, genuine caring for the earth, a caring that extends far beyond the vulgar concern that as we lose 'the environment' we imperil human survival. They not only love nature, beauty, and life but are bold enough to own their anger at their violation and have the heart to empathise with pain. In short, they are dedicated to the wellbeing of life for the sake of life.

By contrast, environmentally-concerned male 'authorities', such as biologist René Dubos (*The Wooing of Earth*, 1980) and environmentalist Barry Commoner (*The Closing Circle*, 1971) reflect in their writing a human-centred bias even as they plead the cause of 'nature'.

I approached Dubos' *The Wooing of Earth* with hopeful curiosity and a great deal of antipathy for the title. I had just finished researching the horrors of animal experimentation. After that, 'wooing the earth' struck an almost cheerful note. However, I was suspicious, for as a woman in patriarchal culture I know that wooing is the kind of gallantry the earth does not need. Even used metaphorically, wooing is a conquering strategy predicated by an active agent on a passive receptacle which is expected to surrender/yield. This understanding is supported by the source of Dubos' title. He took it from a line by the Indian poet Rabindranath Tagore who, upon seeing the European countryside in 1878, wrote of its shapers as men embarked upon a 'heroic love-adventure of the West, the active wooing of the earth'.

The analogy to heroism is telling. Heroic values include an overriding passion to win, subjugate, to seize and hold against someone's will. Heroic deeds occur within the context of 'larger' schemes (wars, games, expeditions) and require either external, 'fated' forces like shipwrecks, enchantments, 'hostile' forces of nature, or elaborate artefacts like rockets and launching pads. 'We' have war heroes, epic heroes, sports heroes, even criminal heroes, real and fictitious men eminently successful in the exercise of violence. Dubos' mind operates on the duality of seduction and heroism implicit in wooing.

At best I found environmental posturing in Dubos' book, never real concern for the earth and even less understanding of basic ecological principles. For example, the comparison of the peasant shaping of the European landscape with such technological feats as the draining of the Zuyder Zee in the Netherlands and the proposed greening of the Arabian desert is a comparison of apples and plastic fruit. There are enormous differences in motivation, experience, and results between the two. For all their ignorance and superstition, the peasants who shaped the European landscape were profoundly attached to the earth. Unheroic but courageous, stubborn and enduring, they practised skills learned from tradition, changing the land slowly, field by field, generation after generation. It is true that many species of plants and animals vanished in the process but the earth was given time to replenish itself and diversify between generations. Besides enriching the depleted soil, rotating crops, recycling wastes – in rural areas, wastes were almost totally organic until World War II – the Europeans loved their land and had eyes for the pleasing, as well as the practical. Hedgerows and meadows, with their incredible variety of plants and grasses, birds and insects, are ecosystems in themselves, beautiful to see and functional as windbreaks, land boundaries, grazing and haying fields.

However, more ambitious enterprises like the draining of the Zuyder Zee to which Dubos refers are technological and massive in design. They are 'scientifically' planned by urbanites emotionally detached from the earth, who will not live and die on the site they are transforming, whose identity is not linked to the daily routine of tending the earth for a lifetime, whose knowledge of soil, plants and animals is technical and abstract, rather than experiential. Like radical surgeons, they alter too much too fast. They lack an appreciation of ecological variables and leave the earth no time to recover, adapt, and diversify. Power and greed motivate them, as they motivate the modern-day European farmers, most of whom have become in the last two decades gross imitators of the abusive agricultural practices employed by their American counterparts. They are no longer peasants, that is, 'of the country', of the land. There is also a misogynistic streak in *The Wooing of Earth*. Dubos sees nature in the same light (or is it obscurity?) as that in which existential philosophers and Jungian psychologists have seen women, that is, as 'potential' unrealised until worked upon by man. Like Sleeping Beauty, nature is immanence, as opposed to transcendence (self-actualising). Like Sleeping Beauty, nature lies in wait for the Prince, whose 'kiss' will awaken her, whose 'love' will bring her to self-realisation. In this case, the Prince is human intervention.

Many of Dubos' statements about human intervention into the natural order beg many questions which to my mind are critical. For example, he writes that: 'The earth has potentialities that remain unexpressed until properly manipulated by human labor and imagination. But [this] also takes love.'[7] Is the Grand Canyon potentially unexpressed? Was the Amazon forest potentially unexpressed until developers started to exploit it by razing such huge tracts of it that *real* environmentalists are now concerned about the oxygen supply to the world? Was the atom potentially unexpressed inside the elements of matter, energising it in harmonious concert? I have purposely chosen examples of awesome proportions, large and small, because they help bring into focus several important questions Dubos passes over. What is *proper* manipulation? Who determines which facets of earth are ready for or need such quickening? What values inform these decisions? And who has the wherewithal to bring about these transformations? It takes a disproportionate share of power, wealth and resources massively to transform nature in ways that are often deleterious to the ecosystem and human wellbeing.

My mind is not put at ease either when I read Dubos' predictions of trends in the 'human relationship between humankind and Earth' to be 'an increasingly centralized management based on the use of highly automated technologies derived from sophisticated science'.[8] I mistrust this impersonal management spawned in laboratories. I mistrust this centralisation of power, data, laws and resources against which the common woman has precious little recourse. As for 'love', what does love mean? Desire to express the 'latent possibilities' of the earth? This is a wooer's love, which presses out what he wants, without taking into consideration the needs of the wooed. To 'love' the earth as potential is equivalent to loving women as potential that remains unexpressed until properly manipulated by man's labour and imagination. 'Love' without reciprocity is exploitation.

The opposite of manipulating nature in order to 'express' it is to leave it alone and assume that nature knows best. Some ecologists hold this view and believe that, as part of nature, people can learn many lessons from observing how she keeps renewing herself without destroying her balance. According to Dubos, 'nature knows best' is a meaningless truism because it leaves out 'the interplay between humankind and the Earth'. For example, people help nature when they tap coal reserves and burn them as fuel and collect guano for use as fertiliser – the accumulation of coal and guano being evidence of nature's 'recycling failures'.

Human failure to understand nature's purpose in such vast storage of natural resources does not mean that nature is failing to complete the recycling process. Coal, oil, peat, guano, etc. are not ecological problems, so utilising them as fuels and fertiliser is not 'a better ecological solution'. All it does is accelerate their return to the life-cycle, but in so doing it empties the cupboard and may even create real ecological problems in the long run. The real immediate problem is that, in making a case for nature's need of human intervention, Dubos rationalises the human will to control.

In addition to 'recycling failures', Dubos adds an example of nature's inadequate methods of keeping its population in check, the better to show that nature does not know best. He cites the population crashes among lemmings and other rodents as a clumsy, ineffective, and painful way to restore the balance between population and food supply. He tells us that the animals suffer before they die. Yes, but so do all creatures caught by predators – a rabbit gripped by a hawk's talons, a frog being slowly swallowed by a snake, an antelope ripped by a lion's claws would probably find it more attractive to die in their sleep, and so would all the innumerable animals under drills, scalpels, needles and electrodes in biological laboratories. In terms of recycling life, as well as species survival, there is nothing clumsy or ineffective about a population crash, which is food for carrion feeders and for the soil. It is presumptuous to label as ineffective on the part of nature any phenomenon humans clumsily fail to understand. Effectiveness is a relative term, in this case measured by human utilitarian criteria. What population crashes demonstrate is that nature has its own design. One might wish that these animals would opt if they could for a less dramatic way of reducing their numbers, for example by regulating their births. (So one might wish for humans, who experience population crashes – wars, plagues, famines – of their own making, not nature's.) The fact that some animals do not conform to our wishes and expectations does not make them clumsy or unwise. On the contrary, it is we who are clumsy and unwise with our incessant translation of nature and her ways into civilised, rational terms.

My most serious objection to *The Wooing of Earth* is that it is steeped in the elitism of a man who manages 'a civilized return to the forest' on his farm in the Hudson Highlands, a scientist who has staked his life in the scientific compound and feels safe from the kind of global control he foresees and welcomes. Dubos' faith in the future is grounded in a conviction that scientists have the knowledge and the wisdom to avert disaster and create a good life. In his words,

> We can create new environments that are ecologically sound, aesthetically satisfying, economically rewarding, and favorable to the continued growth of civilization. But the wooing of the Earth will have a lastingly successful outcome only if we create conditions in which both humankind and the Earth retain the essence of their wildness.[9]

At ease with the most glaring contradictions (a *civilised* forest is not a forest; *manipulated* wildness is no longer wildness), Dubos anticipates both loss and gain of personal freedoms, increased globalisation that will severely curtail one's options and increased decentralisation that could diversify them. If we can judge from history, limited options will affect the technologically ignorant masses while increased options will benefit the privileged few.

The way out of this morass is to strive with all our might to become as independent as possible of those technologies that threaten life on earth. Dubos himself is aware that every technological 'success' has created 'some form of environmental and social degradation'.[10] Yet his faith in technology remains that of 'The Despairing Optimist', as he titles his regular column for *The American Scholar*.

This treacherous optimism is damaging. The message is that the experts know best and the masses are expected blindly to accept their decisions about the 'proper manipulation' of earth. Since industrialists,

scientists, and governments already form vast international conglomerates that control most aspects of our lives, it is easy to
manipulate people into handing personal responsibility over to the experts. All it takes is to inculcate a strong sense of powerlessness in
people while feeding them illusions of individual choice and power.
Once the wooing is over and the reality of a ravished earth sets in, we
might recover our senses and empower *ourselves* again as true lovers,
not wooers, of earth.

I read *The Closing Circle* (1971) by Barry Commoner in 1974, shortly after a feud with neighbours over a modest invasion of dandelions
from my lawn into theirs. Those neighbours were people who like
'weed-free' lawns and want to believe herbicide labels that promise
harmless results after 'careful' application of toxins. I argued in vain.
They killed their dandelions, I kept mine and some months later they
moved to greener turf. I like to think that, if I had read *The Closing
Circle* before these events and used its arguments, they might have
spared their dandelions. Commoner makes it clear that most modern
technological achievements – herbicides among them – are ecological
failures. More importantly, he develops what he named The First
Law of Ecology: Everything is connected to everything else. This,
together with a call for public education and individual choices, are
the chief merits of his book.

Since the publication of *The Closing Circle* much has been made of
the concept of the interconnectedness of all organisms in nature. It is
one of Commoner's virtues to have elaborated the point that
'mankind' is included in the web of interrelated organisms. But are
women included in 'mankind'? He would undoubtedly say yes. Let us
see. In order to stress the credibility of the environmental crisis and
the urgency of his appeal for public involvement, he writes:

> The environmental crisis is hardly a 'motherhood' issue. Nor is it a diver-
> sion from other social questions. For as we begin to act on the en-
> vironmental crisis, deeper issues emerge[11] which reach to the core of our
> system of social justice and challenge basic political goals.[12]

Ecology is very much a motherhood[13] issue since woman and nature
have been linked in our consciousness since prehistory. To delve into
the environmental crisis is to begin to see how fundamental this

connection is to social justice and political goals. Commoner points to blacks and the poor first as primary victims of environmental degradation, then as powerful allies in the fight against it. I would add that all women are victims of degradation. All women are experts in the art of survival.

In 1971 Commoner was aware of the importance of educating the public to the fact that the ecological movement is concerned with survival on a global scale. He suggested making the findings of scientific research accessible to wide audiences by demystifying science and translating data into plain English. He hoped that education would lead to voluntary action, such as wearing unironed cotton shirts to work in order to save energy and boycotting synthetic fabrics as pollutants. I think it is an admirable proposition and I have yet to see it put into practice.

For education to be translated into voluntary action that will make a difference to the quality of life, people must make the connection between abstract research and their personal lives. They must be confronted with the fact that the choices they make directly affect the survival of life on this planet. Nothing short of rebirth into an integral value system will enable the majority to choose consciously and wisely those acts which Commoner hopes will close the circle.

Reading the works of ecologists is maddeningly depressing. The optimism that runs through their pages only serves to add to a general sense of frustration. We are inundated with dismal facts yet repeatedly told that 'we' have finally acquired the knowledge to remedy past failures. It makes one wonder why things are becoming progressively worse. To take the example of plastics, which nowadays are impossible to avoid, it was known before Commoner published his book that they endangered health. 'Animal studies' on chick embryos had shown devastating deformities. Injections of esters of phthalic acid, used in the formulation of polyvinyl chloride plastics, into the yolk sac during embryonic life caused cleft skull, malformed eye, absence of bone tissue, incomplete cornea development, while on hatched chicks they had produced 'tremor, nonpurposeful bodily movement, and a total incapacity of either standing or walking normally'. Commoner adds:

> What is the point of this story? It is NOT reported here in order to suggest that we are all about to perish from exposure to plastic automobile

upholstery. All that can be said at this time about the hazard to health is that there may be one.[14]

Thirteen years later (1984) the Environmental Protection Agency in the USA began considering the removal of the plasticiser DEHP (2-ethylhexyl phthalate) responsible for cancer and deformities in rats, mice, chick embryos, etc.[15] Four years later the EPA is still only *considering* action. Many more animals will be sacrificed while the EPA waits for the results of 'further studies' and many more people will be exposed to the danger of virtually all the 300 million pounds of plastic manufactured per year before the EPA makes a ruling on DEHP. In the absence of strong *human* data, the EPA's decision to restrict the use of DEHP is heavily based on a 'cost/method analysis'. As this plasticiser has been around for a long time providing quality performance (e.g. good bounceability of balls!) at an 'attractive cost', there is a hesitation to take action and 'tie up the plastics industry'.[16] Need I mention that DEHP is only *one* of several noxious plasticisers reported in Commoner's summary. The impression that remains from reading these reports is that far from closing the circle we keep running within it, whether or not 'we' have the knowledge to stop the insane merry-go-round.

In the end, courage is of the essence. I think perhaps the most important role of education today is to combine information with lessons in moral courage: courage not to conform to what information shows is detrimental to life, courage to risk disapproval, to change our lifestyles, to develop those qualities that lie buried in the wasteland of materialism. In this way, writing *The Closing Circle* was an act of courage. Commoner defied many of the 'truths' held sacrosanct by the scientific community and by society at large, especially in 1971, a time in which it had not yet become fashionable to challenge these 'truths'.

The new crusade: conservation

To this new crusade I solemnly pledge what years remain to me.

Jacques Cousteau,
Founder of the Cousteau Society

The new crusaders rally under the banner of conservation in an effort to save the earth from the heretics who exploit it to death. In their rhetoric words like 'Holy Land' have been secularised to express the interconnectedness, rather than the sacredness, of all living organisms. Conservation crusades exude a spirit of zeal and urgency, a sense of a race against time for the preservation of species living in the air, under water, in and above the soil. Thus, they encompass the heavens, the face of the earth, the waters, and the vast underground regions teeming with life we do not see and in whose depths the drama of modern living continues its devastation.

It is important to point out that conservation is built on an inherent flaw, which Aldo Leopold, considered to be the founder of the ecological movement, formulated in 1949: 'All conservation of wildness is self-defeating, for to cherish we must see and fondle, and when enough have seen and fondled, there is no wildness left to cherish.'[17] This is the most distressing aspect of conservation. We need it because its advocates defend the earth in international courts against the rapist mentality that systematically destroys it in the name of progress. However, its educational policies and economic needs make conservation an intrinsic part of the problem it attempts to solve. The human population being disproportionately large, too many people are brought in 'to cherish and fondle', making it necessary for conservation groups to sacrifice either the quality of their educational programmes or the wildlife and the land on which that wildlife depends.

Since conservation is dedicated to keeping the earth in a state of viability, the goals and methods of most groups are similar. I have before me a number of drawers filled with one year's worth of fundraising appeals, special pleas, merchandise catalogues and reports from about twenty organisations to which I do not belong. I also have more detailed literature and regular publications from a handful of others to which I subscribe and pay my dues, not without ambivalence. Most of these groups operate from the 'rational' base they think they need in order to negotiate the compromises they think are realistically possible. Very few of them are involved in direct action.

Greenpeace gained worldwide attention as a direct action group in 1975 when its volunteers stood between the harpoons of a commercial whaler boat and the whale; in 1983 and 1987 its campaigners risked their own safety to plug an underwater pipe discharging radioactive waste from the Sellafield reprocessing plant. These are effective ways to dramatise a problem, raise public awareness, and achieve beneficial results. Such direct actions are not irrational. By allowing feeling to enter reason, the outcome in these instances is courage. If the example of the Greenpeace volunteers was followed by the millions of individuals who care enough about the planet to want to save it, the results would be far quicker and more efficient than those achieved through the conventional negotiation channels used by conservative conservation groups.

What distinguishes the various conservative conservation groups is mainly a question of tone. Some are more sophisticated than others, some more professional and businesslike, some more research oriented. In America all are critical of the Reagan administration's land use, energy policies, and political appointments. They launch campaigns:

to protect 'our wildlife heritage'

to enter public debate on the future of Alaska and provide the voice of conscience

to increase their acreage so that the land 'will be here, as is, for *your* grandchildren'

to lobby against the use of deadly poisons

to save the Environmental Protection Agency

to stop the poaching of Uganda's wildlife 'once and for all'

to support a mutual, verifiable, freeze on the arms race

to stop the legalisation of bear cub slaughter in Pennsylvania

to oppose aerial shooting of wolves in Alaska

to stop the multinational corporations from stripping, dumping, polluting, wasting in 'National Sacrifice Areas'

to pioneer research so that we may better understand the sea and its creatures

to prevent animal abuse before it occurs

to save the whale, the turtle, the sandhill crane, the salamander, the bald eagle, the lady's slipper, the Indian paint brush, the dog tooth violet . . .

and so on.

Conservationists are aware that their crusade is a way of buying time against the steady deterioration of the earth's vital system and its eventual collapse should their recommended conservation measures fail to be implemented. They know that, if all the goals described in their literature were to be achieved tomorrow, new problems would arise which they would need to urgently address. The struggle is endless because society as a whole is governed by destructive, exploitative principles.

Reading the material published by conservation societies leads one to believe that by joining their membership, one captures the Holy Grail and helps preserve the world in pure and radiant splendour. In reality, what we preserve for 'our' children, assuming one is still rash enough to have any, is not nature or the wilderness but man's restructuring of the natural world. I have never liked the word 'preserve' applied outside the realm of jams and jellies. Preserving kills enzymes, 'cures' the growth process, reduces the individual diversity of characteristics, life itself, to a more uniform and manageable mass. Best we leave it to peaches and plums, ripe for the gathering.

Conservation methods include research, education, legal action, political lobbying and the purchase of land. Research and education are problematic. As a conscientious objector to animal research, I want to know beforehand how my dues will be used. I once inquired at the headquarters of the Massachusetts Audubon Society, and, after some waiting in a large general office decorated with stuffed birds, was told in the vaguest of terms that their research consisted of animal, land and pollution studies, which could have meant anything, especially in the presence of those birds. The Cousteau Society mentions the 'formidable intelligence' of dolphins and whales and hopes 'someday to understand the subtleties of their brains'. This sounds very clean. There is no hint of the capture of dolphins and the degrading research done on them to determine, among other things, the degree of their intelligence. Whether the staff of the Cousteau Society are directly involved in this research is of no consequence. What matters is that they support it. These are just two examples among many of the cloud of vagueness and secrecy with which conservation groups protect their research. Since knowledge is power, facts are of course needed to carry the ecological argument to the political, legal and economic arenas with maximum effectiveness. Presumably, lay people should not interfere with their research methods. As a result, those who strongly object to animal research but support the ecological movement face a moral dilemma.

Education is at the heart of conservation but it is fraught with problems. For information to be effective, our whole value system would have to change from the maximisation of profit to the maximisation of the quality of life for all creatures. Thus, ecological facts alone are not likely to change the profit-oriented value system. Facts must be imbued with biophilic values which require first of all a radically different perspective on nature, a new understanding of our place in the natural scheme and a return to habits and feelings which have become lost in the course of technological progress. Conservation is a stop-gap measure precisely because it is grounded in a 'profitable' economy of waste.

We have become wasteful because we no longer have to expend body energy directly to produce the most basic commodities. For example, without running water, we would be in touch with the effort it takes to collect water and the effort alone would make us careful of its use. Without electricity, we would be forced to rise and go to bed early, making more intelligent use of daylight hours, perhaps even discovering again the delights of leisure, imagination and the warmth of human communication. I am not saying that we should restore public wells and candlelight, but that turning a faucet and flipping a switch have made us lazy and thoughtless of our demands on the earth's resources. We not only tolerate intolerable waste of water and electricity, we expect it.

We depend on mass production of crops because we have fled the country and congregate in huge numbers in places where we cannot grow our food. Mass production entails practices that are unhealthy for the soil and destructive of whole ecosystems. Monocropping, chemical fertilisation, fumigants and insecticides are ill-conceived answers to feeding an urbanised population that has placed itself in a state of helplessness and dependency. The alternative to the methods used in mass-producing food are slower and would require a redistribution of land use. Since not enough of us want to face the fact that we cannot continue to live in this way, we entrust our fate to the experts who do *not* know best. We are willing to withstand scandal after scandal. We contribute money to cancer research but passively encourage the proliferation of carcinogens in a crazy, fragmented and mindless way.

Biophilic values mean first of all that we value our lives enough to become responsible. Millions of people everywhere know, at least in theory, what ecologists have demonstrated for over a decade, namely, that if we damage a single link in the ecological circle we damage the whole. This is a sobering thought which, if taken seriously and acted upon, could revolutionise how we perceive ourselves with respect to nature and thus greatly modify our treatment of it. The notion of our rightful stewardship of the earth which man's god mandated in Genesis is divisive. It sets the human species apart from, superior to, and dominant over every other creature. In other words, it gives us the right to objectify nature and do what we please with her. Doing away with this notion would open the way for a reconnecting to nature in kinship. Conservation does not address this issue. In fact, conservationists themselves objectify nature in their pursuit of data, control, management, monitoring, improvement, and so on. Moreover, in an effort to strengthen their financial base, many conservation groups appeal to consumerism by merchandising many superfluous, artfully crafted items, whose nature motifs may enhance our appreciation of nature, but as an 'object to possess'. Besides wasting natural resources, these objects replace the reality of nature with manufactured images. In a shrinking natural world, images may be our only legacy.

Overall, conservation is a necessary good in an unnecessarily evil world. How one chooses to distribute one's resources and energy among the many conservation societies is a matter of personal preference. One can write books, one can join direct action groups – Greenpeace remains undaunted and has moved in many directions since its first intervention on behalf of whales. One can demonstrate with the women at Seneca Falls in the state of New York, at Greenham Common in England, at many peace camps throughout Europe and the United States. One can talk. As a guiding light in our decisions, we can listen to the poets who have as much to say as ecologists do with their facts and figures and educational programming. As Edna St Vincent Millay in 'Afternoon on a Hill' (*Collected Lyrics*) writes:

> I will be the gladdest thing
> Under the sun!
> I will touch a hundred flowers
> And not pick one.

The future of wildlife

> Man did not weave the web of life; He is merely a
> strand in it. Whatever he does to the web, he does to
> himself.
>
> Chief Seattle of the Duwamish Tribe, Washington
> Territory, 1855

Wildlife has no future. Applied to plant and animal life, the word 'wild' means that which grows and lives without regulation or control. Wild means free, and free is a quality 'not determined by anything beyond its own nature or being' (*Websters' New Collegiate Dictionary*). Wildlife can exist only in the wilderness. As we expand into the wilderness, native plants and animals disappear except as they are preserved for their contributions to 'gene banks' and for 'future generations' to see and 'enjoy'. Conservation of wildlife is based on an international plan to capture individuals of those species deemed worthy of being saved from extinction, to confine them in parks, reserves, and aquariums, to control their populations, and to monitor their behaviour. Unless we change the definition of 'wild', to speak of preserving wildlife is a contradiction in terms.

As it is, the dictionary definition of wildlife carries the reduced meaning of 'living things that are neither human nor domesticated: *especially*, mammals, birds, and fishes hunted by man'. This makes conservation of wildlife nothing more than a way to ensure the survival of game and game preserves and does away with the notions of wildlife and wilderness altogether. As we capture, confine, control, cull and kill animals, we strip them of their freedom/wildness. No longer determined by their own nature and being, wildlife has been defined in relation to man-the-predator.

What does this shrinking of the connotative meanings of the word 'wildlife' signify in terms of what we do to ourselves, since what we do to the web, we do to ourselves? We prey on each other, as in crimes and wars. We give up our freedom to think for ourselves and act independently and interdependently. We are no longer wild in the sense in which all animals were once wild, that is, self-regulated and interacting dynamically with a self-regulating environment. As we manage the environment, so we control ourselves following arbitrary social and political directives. We become civilised.

It is interesting to think about what goes into becoming civilised. Looking at the word itself tells us many things, not only about what we have become but also about why there is no future for wildlife. To be civilised, we struck a bargain with the city-state, the *civitas* of ancient Rome that gave us the word 'city' and its derivatives. In exchange for self-regulation (freedom), 'we' received certain rights and privileges – the right to own property, to vote, to receive legal protection, and so on. We became polite, policed, and political, which is the same thing as being civilised, for these words are based on the Greek *polis* (city-state), whose structure the Romans imitated when they founded their *civitas*. We became civil citizens, that is, tamed city-dwellers. We allowed ourselves to be policed by placing ourselves in the position of children in relation to parents, that is, we became civilians belonging to the city-state, the body politic of the metropolis, the mother-city (metro: from Greek, *meter*, mother) controlled by city fathers. Civilisation and wildness do not mix. Civilisation would fall apart if it tolerated freedom (self-regulation, wildness). Wildness cannot assimilate civilisation without being consumed by it.

On the other hand, culture is what every human social organisation has, before it becomes civilised – usually as a result of invasion, conquest, and coercion. At one time, we, too, had a culture similar to that which the Spanish and English invaders found on the American continent when they conquered it. In the culture of the Duwamish chief quoted in the epigraph to these pages, conservation would be as unthinkable a concept as buying or selling land. We are so removed from our origins that we hardly ever think of what we have lost. Rather than re-assessing the values of civilisation, we continue to civilise other cultures considered 'less advanced' because we measure them by our standards. We bring our civilisation to them, not because we want to share a good thing but because it serves our political and economic interests. Is this qualitatively different from how we treat wildlife?

Wildlife has everything to lose whether it is 'allowed' to remain where it belongs (in the wilderness) or whether it is taken to reservations. If it remains, it will eventually lose its habitat under the demands for space of a growing human population and gradually die off. If it is taken to reservations, it will lose its wildness, its self-regulation. In the late 1940s, Aldo Leopold wrote that conservation practices are 'to a large extent, local alleviations of biotic pain. They are necessary, but they must not be confused with cures.'[18] Is the biotic pain of the animal inmates at the 6,000 square mile area in Tanzania (the Serengeti National Park) alleviated by their confinement? Overcrowded and closely watched, the animals must also contend with ogling tourists in motor vehicles, prowling game wardens, and zoologists on the research trail. Roughly the size of Hawaii, the park hosts more than 1,150,000 animals expected to live 'in natural conditions'.[19]

This is a non-future for wildlife. If we manage to stop destroying the earth, it is likely that most land surfaces will someday look like the United States and much of Europe with their concentrated production centres, densely populated cities, tentacular suburbs, and endless expanses of tarmac, covering what was once the wilderness. There will be the usual abundance of pets which will add a predatory threat to the remaining 'wildlife'. There will be zoological 'gardens' and aquariums, national parks and sanctuaries where, for a fee, 'wild' animals can be viewed. Everything else will be *pre-served* in museums, in special collections of dead – and extinct – species. The image of once-living, free-ranging animals will be preserved as motifs on T-shirts, cups, trays, towels, calendars, greeting cards, etc. The song of birds that will awaken one in the morning will be recorded and broadcast over the radio, or captured on cassettes such as the 'Audible Audubon' that one can take into the surrounding man-made environment. Popular television series like National Geographic Specials, and speciality shows in which organised, scientific information abounds, will be the closest approximation people will have of the natural world. Many people will miss the wilderness. Everywhere, those who do will scramble for whatever land remains, yearning to return to 'the simple life', in direct contact with living trees and flowers and animals but, above all, in search of self-regulation and control of the quality of their lives. Multitudes will support all kinds of conservancies in an effort to preserve their treasured 'natural' heritage for their children's children.

How to determine the ground rules for the new conservation ethics necessary to accommodate the animals invaded by civilisation has been under consideration for a number of years. In *The Cult of the Wild*, Boyce Rensberger attempts to shatter the myths about wild animals so that sound conservation measures may be drawn up unhampered by sentimentalism and irrational misconceptions. He presents what he likes to call an objective, mature, and realistic picture of current arguments as well as an assessment of the new conservation ethics being formulated on an international scale by a number of large conservation groups. His position conforms to our cultural prejudice of placing the human animal at the top of all created things and valuing all others according to their usefulness to us. It narrows objectivity down to objectification in which self-interest and utilitarianism play a key role in determining conservation policies.

For example, in his review of the ecological argument that all organisms contribute to the wholesomeness of the biosphere; damage to one weakens all others, Rensberger agrees that organisms at the bottom of 'the food chain' are essential to the life process. However, he does not see any survival value *for human beings* in the protection of animals at the top of the chain, such as the whooping crane, the African elephant, or the Sumatran rhinoceros. This may be true, but there is more to life than human survival. From a moral point of view, those animals were here first and we have not the right to play god and decide their fate. Moreover, without presuming to enter the brain of crane, elephant, rhinoceros to determine how they feel about being pushed out of existence, it is quite clear that an animal starving because its food supply is no longer adequate, or an animal thwarted in its instincts for survival by any or all of the conditions we have created around it, is an animal in the state of 'biotic pain' for which we are responsible.

The aesthetic argument for conservation focuses on the intangible rewards of feeling oneself in harmony with nature by spending time alone in it. This, too, is a people-centred argument and, like the ecological one, is in itself harmless to animals. It is this aesthetic sense that enabled David Thoreau and, in our own time, Annie Dillard, to enrich their experience of life and transmit their gift to their readers. Communion with nature requires not only time, curiosity, and the desire to observe, but the space in which to be alone with it. Rensberger appreciates the aesthetic argument, in which he includes 'the educational value of animals', that is, scientific study for practical benefits. Moreover, he points out the problem of defining what is meant by 'aesthetics'. In so far as aesthetic values are cultural, what is pleasing in one culture may be a nuisance in another. For example, a tourist may 'thrill' to the sight of lions but to a Masai tribesman trying to raise cattle, lions are dangerous pests. I would argue that thrill is not necessarily a matter of aesthetics, that tourists are notoriously insensitive to aesthetics, and that it is up to the Masai tribesman to see how he can tend his cattle and deal with lions without destroying either one. The human problem with lions and elephants is really economic and political, not aesthetic.

Given the utilitarian values that have spread like wildfire everywhere, the economic argument for conservation is likely to be the one which is most persuasive to most people. It is based on the principle that ways must be found to have the animals 'pay for their keep' and in addition, bring economic gains to people. Among the profit-making suggestions are the 'harvesting' and selling of animal products, such as meat, hides, ivory, etc. All of this comes under the rubric of controlled cropping. Tourism is another, though less attractive, possibility, since the revenues from tourism typically go to rich entrepreneurs, most of whom are foreigners. And finally, there is the proposition that, since the wealthy West is the one to insist that large tracts of land in developing countries like Africa be given over for the conservation of wild animals, it should pay for it. It makes eminent sense that if Africans are deprived of their land and its products so that the West can achieve its conservation goals, the Africans ought to be compensated in cash and food supplies. This is an old story – the West is dictating, once again, how the rest of the world should live – and certainly is not limited to Africa. According to Rensberger, much foreign capital is behind the large-scale deforestation of southeast Asia and the South American Amazon rain forest, causing the destruction of irreplaceable and indispensable ecosystems. The timber and beef derived from these projects are, to a large extent, destined for consumption in the West. A renewed form of colonialism springs from conservation for economic gain – more insidious than the old, but every bit as destructive and unjust.

Thus the new conservation ethic is moving in the direction of economics. Rensberger reports that controlled cropping and the assigning of monetary value to animals are the preferred ways to determine who is to be saved, but that their implementation is hindered by the reluctance of international conservation groups to publicise their deliberations on the matter for fear of alienating their membership who, on the whole, lack 'a mature appreciation of wild animals'. In this connection, I am reminded that in 1980 the Massachusetts Audubon Society informed its membership that it regretfully supported the US

Fish and Wildlife Service proposal to poison gulls on Monomy Island in order to 'increase the chances of survival of the tern colony'. They reasoned as follows: 'Since we know that the increase in gull numbers is the direct result of human activities, particularly the increase in the number of open garbage dumps, we feel that it is not only appropriate but imperative that we safeguard other members of the wildlife community that might suffer from this increase.'[20] This is a form of controlled cropping. The solution to this problem might have taken another route if Massachusetts Audubon had joined forces with the US Fish and Wildlife Service and other groups to pressure cities and towns to eliminate open garbage dumps, or better yet, to encourage people to recycle their wastes. This example illustrates that the membership *is* acquainted with its organisation's stands on controlled cropping, hunting and so on.

According to Rensberger, it is too late to adopt a hands-off policy that would leave nature to recover by itself from the toxins we have poured into it, and from the degree of habitat destruction we have wrought. He writes:

> Some form of wildlife management will be necessary to offset the disruption already caused by human competition and the disruptions that will continue simply because most protected areas are likely to have artificial boundaries.[21]

This may be true. However, the desire to leave nature alone does not spring from 'false and sentimental notions about animals', as he would have us believe. If being human means anything, the least we can do is learn to respect the integrity of life and to live intelligently, with our eyes set on goals larger and more wholesome than 'management'. As Dorothy Wordsworth wrote (in 'Peaceful Our Valley, Fair and Green'):

—Beside that gay and lovely rock
    There came with merry voice
A foaming stramlet glancing by,
    It seemed to say 'Rejoice!'

My youthful wishes all fulfilled
    Wishes matured by thoughtful choice,
I stood an Inmate of this vale,
    How could I but rejoice?

Space colonies: the great escape

Overpopulation and the rate of consumption of the earth's goods combined with pollution problems and mismanagement of natural resources have led many to suggest that the human species and nature as we know them are coming to an end. The response to this impending apocalypse depends upon investment and education. Most people ignore it because it is made easy to ignore, shrouded as it is in a false notion of progress. When we look around us, we see the convenience of a major highway intersection or a new shopping mall rather than the loss of woodland, rocks or arable land, all of them hosts to a variety of animals and plants to which we never gave a thought. Moreover, we see none of the genetic mutations and withering of life that presage disaster. People look the same as they always have. The birds and bees are still there. We feel reassured by the predictability of spring. We go on ordering seeds and planning our gardens.

Except in the event of a nuclear holocaust, the earth's systems will not collapse overnight. However, life-threatening damages are everywhere. We can shut them out of our minds because in an urbanised world where the opinion-makers live, people have lost their vital connection to nature. Experience has been replaced by mediated images that mirror the cultural perception of nature as a commodity to enjoy and to use. Advertising and television package nature to attract the consumer with the message that it is fun, never endangered. Technological magic whips corn into tacos and wheat into bread in a trice, juxtaposing the products with close-ups of 'nature' for television viewers who have never seen a corn- or wheatfield and are ignorant of – or do not care about – the ecological damage caused by the methods of modern agriculture.

However, the damage is brought into the full light of publicity when it is too late. I suspect this is a political strategy whereby 'solutions' which would have raised a storm of protests are manipulated to appear essential, even unavoidable. This is the case with NASA's proposed space laboratory which the Reagan administration approved in January 1984 and sold to the American public as an enterprise capable of 'lifting' the nation into a new era of prosperity. Thus described in the vaguest terms, the space laboratory, which has existed on drafting boards for many years, is about to be realised.[22] This can be seen as a preparatory step toward the launching of colonies in space, which also exist on drafting boards and for which much research and many experiments are being conducted. In other words, space colonies are projected as the ultimate 'solution' to a burned-out earth. Space colonies may be good material for science fiction, having at least the virtue of exercising the imagination. For years we have been served a diet of fictitious out-to-get-you aliens, monsters born of fear and intended to fuel the notion that the unknown is frightening. Now as space travel and colonies move from the realm of fantasy into reality, it is interesting to note that a recent alien fad has taken a sharp turn from the beaten path of horror and hazards. E.T. is an envoy of goodwill and love, a spokesperson of humanitarian values. This changing image taps human longings for a better life but, since nothing is accidental in this super-mediated world, it also serves to shape a more positive attitude toward the unknown reaches of space as the latest wilderness slated for human colonisation.

No one can describe space colonies better than physicist Gerard O'Neill who proposed and engineered them on paper. For him, these colonies differ from classical utopias in conception, means, and design. Utopias and communes conformed to 'rigid social ideas' and suffered from 'restricted technology'. On the other hand, space colonies are characterised by 'the opening of new social possibilities to be determined by the inhabitants, with the help of a basically new technological methodology, on the part of the space communities'.[23] The new social possibilities will arise from experimenting freely, 'in isolation from planetary hangups'. The new technological methodology is given more coverage in O'Neill's scheme for space colonies, perhaps because men find it easier to speak about hardware, perhaps because of their limited and rigid understanding of 'social possibilities'.

As a beginning, 'we' will leave behind all the parasitic species on which man poured his poisons in a vain effort to eradicate them and 'we' will take along 'those species which we want' – an occasional pet and 'meat animals' such as chickens, turkeys, and pigs. Will agriculture drain the new environment as it drained the earth? It will not. Extraterrestrial farming in the new environment will be practised in rotating 'space drums' with the technological assistance of artificial lighting, nutrient sprayings, hydroponics and controlled weather and climate conditions. Since plants do not need 'visual amenities', they will grow very nicely in the sterile chambers of space islands.

In the same spirit, the mining of natural resources will not destroy or pollute because they will take place on the Moon and the asteroid belt where nobody lives. Nuclear power plants? By all means, but they can be located safely on the Moon also. The effects of zero gravity and cosmic ray radiation pose no serious problem to the organism because technology can solve anything in a virgin environment. As for the space dwellers' possible difficulty of adaptation to the strangeness of their new environment, no one needs to worry. They will be psychologically 'well equipped' for long space journeys and long residence in space.

Who will these space dwellers be? Speaking to an International Symposium on the Future of Man held in London in the late 1960s, the world-renowned geneticist J.B.S. Haldane described the ideal future type:

> A gibbon is better suited than a man for life in a low gravitational field, such as that of a space-ship, an asteroid, or perhaps even the moon. A platyrrhine with a prehensile tail is even more so. Gene grafting may make it possible to incorporate such features into the human stock.[24]

Since the participants of this Symposium took extraterrestrial environments and modified human forms for granted, Haldane could give his imagination free rein. He suggested the breeding of legless astronauts, adding that 'a regressive mutation to the condition of our ancestors in the mid-Pliocene, with prehensile feet, that can grasp things, no appreciable heels and an ape-like pelvis, would be still better.'[25] In the event 'we' should want to live in the high gravitational fields of the planet Jupiter, the ideal creatures would be quadrupeds 'with short legs and squat bodies'. For Jupiter, Haldane would 'back an achondroplastic against a normal man'. This achondroplastic is a technological monster and a man is a man.

The horror of these monsters is not so much *the idea* of combining 'subhuman' with human creatures* and inserting electronic devices

---

* Hybrid monsters have existed in the human *imagination* since time immemorial. Like Gorgons, Medusas and the like, they served an intensely religious function, which in all 'primitive' cultures, was also intensely social. This blending of animal and human forms resulted from human identification with animals. Icarus and Mary Shelley's *Frankenstein* serve as warnings about the consequences of mixing such imaginings with hubris.

in humans but rather in the motivation, techniques and intended results that are implicit in the idea. The horror is in the actual violation of the integrity of life of millions of animals who suffer in laboratory experiments so that the techniques for assembling these monsters can be perfected. So far, the best-known techniques comprise grafting, cell fusion, organ transplants, and implantation of electronic devices into living organisms. Some scientists predict that those of us alive in the year 2025 will see the first human–animal hybrids. The horror resides in the creation of a new slave population composed of creatures ideally suited for space travel and extra-planetary explorations, creatures immune to radioactivity, creatures with pre-set 'life'-spans, performing set tasks, fulfilling a variety of functions, including serving as donors in organ transplant 'farms'.

The robotisation of life, of which the above is but an extreme form, is nothing new, but it seems to me that it takes people morbidly alienated from feeling to draw such blueprints of space colonies. According to some scientific geniuses, we even need the help of machines to tell us what we feel. Dr Joe Kamiya of the San Francisco Langley Porter Neuropsychiatric Institute suggests that in the twenty-first century, it will be possible to mediate emotions with machines. Somewhere, someone may sit in an armchair and play a musical instrument controlled by brain waves conducted through electrodes pasted to *his* head, which will enable *him* to hear *his* moods as *he* would hear a symphony: 'He would lead his own orchestra, so to speak. He would feel himself.' What about lovers? They 'would be freed of the difficulties *people* so often have when they try to express their emotions in words. They could flirt through their brain waves.' Best of all, children attached to biofeedback machines would 'learn that when they have certain emotions, their palms sweat'.[26]

Maybe I am too earth-bound. Maybe I love this earth the way it is, with its insects and weeds, rains and cold spells. Maybe it is because I know what I feel when my palms sweat. Whatever the reason, I find space colonies an outrageous proposition, belonging to the nether regions beyond hell and fallen angels, stagnating in rank amorality. If that is the future, I resist it, which does not mean I resist change. As Louis J. Halle, Professor Emeritus at the Graduate Institute of International Studies in Geneva, Switzerland, would have it, resistance to change, in this case to space colonies, comes from having too narrow a concept of 'mankind', too limited a view of natural selection. For him, evolution itself is petering out as if, having exhausted her creative energy, nature had called out to man that she could do no more and man, forced to survive on his own, had outwitted her for the last time. For the outcome of this last evolutionary pressure upon the fittest is in effect a last goodbye to nature. Turning his back on her, man gives birth to himself. As Halle states, like the frog and the chickadee, survival depends on the achievement of complete independence from the environment.[27]

Indeed, the narrow view in all of this is his view of the frog and the chickadee, which have admirably adapted to new conditions in their environment without recourse to technology. The ability to design and implement colonies in space does *not* create independence from the earth's environment. Until such time as we are made of another substance, the earth *is* our environment. To argue that the genetic mutations and mind control devices necessary for 'life' in space are as natural as the evolution of the frog in its 'transcendence' from water to land, is to bypass the evolutionary *process* whereby myriads of miniscule mutations developed in concert with all organisms to 'produce' the frog. To say with Halle and others, that if human beings had already evolved '350 million years ago, [they] would have been horrified at the thought that life was about to expand onto dry land'[28] is to fall into the dull anachronism of projecting today's consciousness on to the minds of imaginary hominids. The statement also omits the fact that man-made mutations are artificial, restricted, and controlled while expansion on to dry land evolved very slowly by natural – not artificial – selection within the earth's atmosphere to which water and land animals belong.

Even in his most outlandish dreams, man depends on 'the environment'. The humanisation of space, as O'Neill calls the new venture, relies heavily on the technician's ability to create the illusion of earth. In the space colonies, rotation will *simulate* gravity, the environment will be earth*like*, the 'sky' will be blue through the manipulation of light and artfully placed mirrors. To a man–machine and to someone deprived of discernment because of conditioning, genetics, and surgery, illusion may be enough. I still call it dependence on the earth's environment.

Having seen what lies in store for 'life' in space colonies, we can reconsider O'Neill's original distinctions between his extraterrestrial scheme and historical utopias: the degree of technology and social possibilities. The inhabitants of space colonies will certainly have a battery of technologies available to them which were not available to the participants in the utopian communes. What advantage this will be for the 'success' of space colonies is questionable as these technologies are mere elaborations and adaptations to space of land contraptions and power transmission devices that reflect the exploitative mentality that has been with us for a long time. The scheme of 'new social possibilities' for the space colonies duplicates the affluent white man's concept of the 'good life': 'happy space dwellers . . . among swimming pools, artificial rivers, clubrooms and sumptuous terraced apartments overlooking pest-free, climate-controlled agricultural rings'.[29] However, the colonisation of space *is* fundamentally different from historical utopias because it is utterly devoid of a sense of personal responsibility and a religious ideal which, however imperfectly they were put into practice, nevertheless inspired the utopian communities to return to nature, grow roots, develop aesthetic sensitivity and relate to life.

The utopian flight from materialism has often been interpreted as an escape, implying that the person or the group is unable to face reality and chooses to run from it. As such, escapism is one of the big *don'ts* in this culture suggesting nonconformity bordering on treason or insanity. However, when O'Neill refers to the 'humanisation' of space as an *escape* from the limits to hope, experimentation, diversity, and personal freedom, he is evoking a positive image. I fail to see in his space colonies the positive element that characterises utopian communities – namely, life-enhancing values. There is nothing transcendent about the values that motivated NASA to have astronauts lodge an identification plaque on the moon indicating that men had landed there. This gesture grates as much as coming upon a tree or a rock defaced with 'John loves Mary' or some similar nonsense in a supposedly wilderness area. Now that the emphasis is shifting away from exploration and toward commercial and military uses of outer space there can be no further doubt that competition, materialism, consumerism and power politics will board the space ships.[30] There is really no difference between the 'humanisation' of space and the colonisation of Africa or Latin America.

Myth historian Joseph Campbell has great expectations for the colonisation of space. He sees Earthrise (the Earth rising above the horizon of the Moon as seen by the Apollo 10 astronauts in 1969) as 'the dawning of a new spiritual awareness', i.e. Mother Earth united with 'Father' Sky. As a symbol it calls us to free ourselves from bondage to the past and be born into the new order of things. The new order is marked by unity since there are no horizons or divisions in the vastness of outer space. More concretely, the divisions between in-groups and out-groups must disappear and be replaced by a recognition of our common humanity. Likewise we can no longer think in terms of heaven and earth as being separate because we have *seen* that the earth is in heaven. Thus, we must embrace the space age as 'we' embraced other redemptory symbols like Easter, the Cross, or the Assumption of the Virgin Mary.[31]

Campbell is speaking from the patriarchal perspective where divisions between good/evil, body/soul, superior/inferior have been symbolised by male gods residing above common mortals. I want to know why women, people of colour and the poor should embrace yet another symbol from the hands of their male, white, affluent, militaristic oppressors. After all, Earthrise as an experience, and ultimately as a symbol, was made possible only by standing on the backs of these 'out-groups'. I say this not with the intention of clinging to the spirit of 'exclusivity' which has created rifts and hostility among people. For me, the Earthrise we are now able to see symbolises the re-emergence into human consciousness of our ancient ties of unity with the earth, her creatures and her cosmic potencies.

Space exploration may bring valuable information leading to a better understanding of the solar system. It may even bring co-operation between hostile nations. However, without a thorough overhaul of human values before we get there, the colonisation of space will merely transport our 'planetary hang-ups' somewhere else. The blueprints for those future colonies give no indication that values have changed. They show no respect for the new environment, no wider acceptance of life, no aspirations toward transcendence. They repeat the worst habits and prejudices that plague earth societies.

The eagerness to escape 'planetary hang-ups' is the eagerness to escape the patriarchal hang-up about life. To see life on earth as confinement amounts to being unable to live life. The paradox in this case is that to escape confinement it is necessary to create it. Images of space travel and space islands are images of physical confinement and regressivism to an infantile state of dependency. In the space ship, the hose attached to the traveller's suit is the umbilical cord, the traveller's support system. Or, as in O'Neill's vision, individuals freely moving in the controlled environment of space bubbles are encased in a kind of plastic womb. However, the mother function is absorbed in the mechanical just as the rocket's probe into space asserts a mechanical power over mother/nature. Whether these ships and islands eventually achieve less crude conditions is irrelevant. Future life in space will still be confined by the closed system of the capsule, the space suit, the space island. Colonies in space are the ultimate escape from nature, the ultimate utopia – nowhere. (*Utopia* comes from the Greek *ou*, not, no; *topos*, place.)

Historically, our destiny as women and the destiny of nature are inseparable. It began within earth/goddess-worshipping societies which celebrated the life-giving and life-sustaining powers of woman and nature, and it remains despite our brutal negation and violation in the present. Women must re-member and re-claim our biophilic power. Drawing upon it we must make the choices that will affirm and foster life, directing the future away from the nowhere of the fathers to the somewhere that is ours – on this planet – now.

Notes

1. Susan Griffin, *Woman and Nature: The Roaring Inside Her* (New York: Harper & Row, 1978; London: The Women's Press, 1984), p.219.
2. Rachel L. Carson, *The Sea Around Us* (New York: New American Library, 1961; London: Willian Collins, 1960), p.93.
3. Rachel L. Carson, *Silent Spring* (New York: Fawcett World Library, 1962; Harmondsworth: Penguin Books, 1982), p.83.
4. Louise B. Young, *Earth's Aura* (New York: Avon Books, 1979; Harmondsworth: Penguin Books, 1982), p.257.
5. In the same sound, sane and shocking tradition, Dr Rosalie Bertell offers a thorough and current account of the plight of life on this already highly radioactive planet. See *No Immediate Danger: Prognosis for a Radioactive Earth* (London: The Women's Press, 1985). She documents the interconnections between harnessing nuclear energy for 'peaceful' purposes and harnessing nuclear energy for military purposes, exposing how they feed off each other and how they *both* move us toward the same deadly outcome. She uncovers rationalisations, lies, secrecy . . . which officials employ to numb public awareness and sensitivity to what is *really* going on and to the real costs of any nuclear endeavours. And even though her perspective is not a radical feminist one, Dr Bertell names and discusses the necessary, urgent, key role of women, 'who have not

become so unnaturally separated from their instincts' (p.374) to constitute the vanguard in 'uprooting war from home and school' (p.377) and effecting the revolution to peace.

5. Dr Helen Caldicott, *Nuclear Madness: What You Can Do!* (Brookline, Mass.: Autumn Press, 1978), p.83.

7. René Dubos, *The Wooing of Earth* (New York: Charles Scribner's Sons, 1980; London: Athlone Press, 1980), p.xv.

8. ibid., p.156.

9. ibid., p.159.

10. ibid., 'Appendix II. Selected successes and associated problems of the technological/industrial era', p.162.

11. It must not be assumed that writing in 1971 before the spread of feminism is responsible for the trivialisation of woman implied in Commoner's statement. In December 1983 the ecological group Friends of the Earth published a spate of letters to the editor in their magazine *Not Man Apart*. Someone had objected to the word 'Man' as sexist in that context and therefore not befitting an organisation dedicated to the well-being of the whole planet. A generous half of those letters dismissed the objection as *trivial* and *unworthy* of serious consideration on the grounds that ecology in general and Friends of the Earth in particular had more pressing and *intelligent* things to do than haggling over a word.

12. Barry Commoner, *The Closing Circle: Nature, Man and Technology* (New York: Bantam Books, 1972; London: Jonathan Cape, 1972), p.209.

13. For a discussion of motherhood as institutionalised mothering, see Adrienne Rich, *Of Woman Born: Motherhood as Experience and Institution* (New York: W.W. Norton & Company, 1976; London: Virago, 1977).

14. Commoner, *The Closing Circle*, p.229.

15. James S. Poles, '"New-Car" Smell May Be Hazardous to Your Health', *Not Man Apart*, 14 (2) (February-March 1984), p.5.

16. Conversation with EPA employee in toxic chemicals, Boston, 7 November 1987. In this same conversation it was also 'suggested' that if one were a manufacturer of vinyl toys for children one should use something else.

17. Aldo Leopold, *The Sand County Almanac* (New York: Oxford University Press, 1966), p.108

18. ibid., p.274.

19. To be sure, there are behavioural aberrations in the animals of the Serengeti National Park, as there are among people living under similarly crowded and invaded conditions. It has been observed that in *three* years, there have been fourteen killings of a lion by another. To science reporter of *The New York Times*, Boyce Rensberger, from whom I took the above

statistic, this is a high incidence of violence. To match it, people would have to kill each other at above the annual US murder rate of 9 or 10 per 100,000. Using this, together with zoologist Dian Fossey's observations that 15 per cent of the gorilla's interactions are violent, Rensberger throws the myth of the beastliness of man out of the window. For to equal the violence of Fossey's gorillas, people would have to hurt one another on every eighth interaction and, according to him, they do not. See Boyce Rensberger, *The Cult of the Wild* (Garden City, New York: Anchor Books, 1978), pp.186–7, 200. However, by my own reckonings, which include wars, rape, and a multitude of abusive acts daily committed against women, children, *and* animals, man is very far from being 'among the most pacific of the large animal species'.

20. *Massachusetts Audubon*, 19 (10) (July 1980), p.12.
21. Rensberger, *The Cult of the Wild*, p.219.
22. In 1976, NASA commissioned a task group 'to identify and examine the various possibilities for the civil program over the next twenty-five years' (NASA SP–386, 'Outlook for space: report to the NASA administrator by the Outlook for Space Study Group', Scientific and Technical Information Office, Washington, DC, 1976, p.iv). Among the recommendations: the use of space to predict and monitor climate and severe weather, crop production, water availability and changes in the environment; to generate energy for the earth; to dispose of hazardous wastes; to study 'the effects of gravity on the evolution and forms of terrestrial life as well as the effects on human beings living and working in space for extended periods of time' (p.96). They discussed the inevitable consequences of this co-operative space effort, namely, the loss of autonomous government in the cities and towns and the incorporation of states into federal rule. In 1983 and 1984, some of these proposals came up for debate. For example, conservation groups and concerned scientists are fighting against the disposal of nuclear waste in space. No one has as yet related the totalitarianism which NASA's enforced co-operation entails to the totalitarian state Orwell described in his novel *1984*. Economist Robert Heilbroner has stated categorically that in this overpopulated world survival is impossible except at 'the fearful price' of coercion, loss of personal freedom and severe limitation of options characteristic of autocratic societies. Is this what we want?
23. Gerard K. O'Neill, *The High Frontier: Human Colonies in Space* (New York: William Morrow & Co.: 1977; London: Corgi Books, 1978), pp.200–1.
24. See David Rorvik, *As Man Becomes Machine* (New York: Pocket Books, 1978; London: Souvenir Press, 1973), p.147.
25. ibid.
26. Maya Pines, *The Brain Changers: Scientists and the New Mind Control*

(New York: Harcourt Brace Jovanovich, 1973; London: Allen Lane, 1974), pp.65–6.

27. Louis J. Halle, 'Our imminent colonization of space', *Harvard Magazine*, 81 (4) (March–April 1979), pp.43–6.
28. ibid., p.46.
29. David Gelman, with Sharon Begley, William Cook and Louise Alexander, 'Colonies in Space', *Newsweek*, 27 November 1978, p.96.
30. John Noble Wilford, 'Big business in space', *The New York Times Magazine*, 18 September 1983, pp.47, 50, 83–5, 86.
31. Eugene Kennedy, 'Earthrise: the dawning of a new spiritual awareness', *The New York Times Magazine*, 15 April 1979, pp.14–15, 51–6.

Epilogue
Andrée M. Collard (1926–1986):
A Biophilic Journey

I met Andrée Collard in 1979 when she was delivering an impassioned lecture on the violation of nature, animals and women to Mary Daly's class on Feminist Ethics. Shortly thereafter we began working together on Rape of the Wild *and eventually came to realise our mutual dream of homesteading on a small piece of land in Norwell, Massachusetts.*

Born in Brussels, the oldest in a family where sons were trained for business and daughters for marriage, Andrée was raised in a village in the French-speaking part of Belgium and remained there until after World War II. It was in the lap of this European countryside with its blend of the aesthetic and the practical, the wild and the domesticated, the sturdy and the delicate, that her intelligent passion for nature was nourished and her outrage at nature's destruction was forged. Andrée's identification with nature was complete – when nature hurt, *she* was in pain. When nature throbbed, *she* was in ecstasy. When nature was violated, *she* was enraged. This tangible and spiritual kinship with the earth and her creatures and elements sustained Andrée's soul and provided her with an inner strength which guided her throughout her days.

As a child, Andrée spent hours walking the woods exploring for anial footprints, fossilised rocks, rare mosses, berries, mineral water springs, sour clover. She never lost her exhilaration and gratitude at being a witness to the marvels of nature and a participant in the sacredness of life.

Her tenderness towards nature was matched by her fury at man's irresponsible intrusion into and violation of the life and wellbeing of animals. She early recognised and acted upon a fact to which she later returned in her writing – animals do not need to be liberated in the sense that, for example, women and blacks must liberate themselves from their oppressed mentality as well as from their oppressors. Animals, having no oppressed mentality, simply need to be *freed*. And so as a child she fought boys in the act of stoning animals – mostly squirrels and frogs – and thwarted the attempts of the village men engaged in their favourite pastime: luring and trapping wild birds in order to cage them. She beat the bushes to flush the birds away from the snares of the men waiting in ambush. The men were always livid and Andrée learned to run very fast. Once she managed to release all the birds from twenty cages that hung, as status symbols, on the front wall of a village house. Never one to tolerate the intolerable, no matter what the consequences to herself, she persisted in her confrontational politics whenever she encountered such abuses.

World War II brought drastic changes to the lives of people living in occupied Belgium, one of which was severe food shortages. The garden Andrée tended quickly became a necessity as the food she produced became the mainstay of the family larder. She recalled those days as filled from morning to night with strenuous physical labour and constant vigilance. The very air was charged with the daily struggle for basic survival and with the ominous presence of the Nazis.

From 1940–4, Andrée was active in the underground resistance movement. The dense forests and wild countryside of wartime Belgium provided a natural refuge and cover for allied soldiers who were caught in occupied territory and were attempting to escape to England. Andrée was frequently their guide, leading them to her village and eventually escorting them through the woods to the next underground resistance unit en route to safety. She also regularly carried messages from one outpost to another in the hollow bars of her bicycle. Several times the Nazis did stop and search her, but they never discovered the hiding place. There would have been dire consequences if they had.

Four years after the war, burning to seek her fortune in the 'continent of golden opportunities', Andrée boarded a freighter bound for New Orleans. Her parents had offered her a 'choice' between marriage and secretarial school and she had refused. She left behind voices full of criticism and fears and predictions that she would fail. In 1945, a girl did not go off on her own, especially to an unknown world full of predatory males. Besides, she did not know English and did not even have a high school diploma (her high school education had been interrupted by frequent bombing and the vicissitudes of life in an occupied country). Andrée's cabin mate, a highly educated chemist, suggested that she settle in Houston, Texas, and go to college. Her support and assistance saw Andrée through the most difficult times there, where she learned enough English to find a parttime job and study at the University of Texas.

Two years later, wanting to learn Spanish and to see more of the world, Andrée was on her way to Mexico on scholarship to complete her BA degree in Romance Languages. She faced life alone in this new land, exciting and utterly foreign to what she had known before. Thrown back again on her own resources, she studied, travelled, learned of the people and was enthralled with the lushness and tranquillity of pre-industralised Mexico.

Several years later, BA in hand, Andrée arrived in New York City to find a teaching job and test herself in still another new land. But the BA did not open doors for her as she had expected and she found herself penniless at the YWCA. Her discouragement was severe; the old voices tolling failure resounded in her ears. Yet she knew she either made it on her own now or returned defeated to the 'security' of home in Belgium. She took a job she hated as an interpreter. In two years, she had saved enough money to return to Mexico and earn a master's degree there. In 1958, she returned to the States and enrolled in the Ph.D programme at Harvard.

Andrée spent her first year at Harvard in a compensatory frenzy of book-learning. Between her unfinished high school education, her immigrant status, her country ways and her insecurity with the language, she was plagued by the terror of being thought a fraud. Very few women were enrolled in the Harvard graduate schools at that time and of those who entered with her, Andrée alone finished the degree. She recalled the experience as intensely lonely and potentially utterly dehumanising save for the support system the women created among themselves.

Yet this was but a foretaste of what she experienced as a faculty member at Brandeis University. She was at Brandeis in 1969 when the second wave of feminism roared through American campuses. Finally a vocabulary with which to name and understand oppression began to emerge. No longer silent, no longer internalising non-existent inferiorities, Andrée confronted the enemy now made plainly visible. With courage and daring, she emerged from the ranks of the invisible and 'came out' not only as a radical feminist but also as a lesbian.

Feminism with its ideals and activism and bonding in strength with women was another new land for Andrée, only this time it was not strange, it was not alien. It was coming home after a long enforced absence, a coming more solidly into her own after being blocked by a shadow. Her 'homecoming' was filled with group consciousness-raising and activism (Andrée was one of the founding members of the Boston chapter of N.O.W.).

Andrée fought long and hard to have the voice and experience of women heard and valued in her sphere of influence. She was one of the first to propose new courses and general curriculum reform, all of which were defeated, and all of which had the effect of getting her labelled, harassed, undervalued, underpaid, and underpromoted. In 1971 she chaired the faculty committee to investigate the status of women at Brandeis. Andrée also established and managed an on-campus office, 'Women and Career Options', under a grant from the Carnegie Foundation. And she finally received approval for her 'Women in Literature' course which she taught passionately and radically to classes packed with students.

Curriculum reform, watch-dog committees, and affirmative action policies brought surface changes to the visibility of women on campus, yet Andrée knew that liberal was not radical, tokenism was not liberation, and assimilation was not revolution. With anger and bitter disappointment, she moved into the dangerous, lonely land of 'the boundary'. Yet, despite reprimands, harassment, overt and covert hostility, she never relinquished her freedom of thought and expression, her belief in herself.

Andrée always spoke her mind as honestly and forcefully as she could, refusing to be silenced by guilt over 'hurting someone's feelings'. She believed that guilt was a totally useless emotion which can be eliminated by taking responsibility. Awareness. Responsibility. These had long been her routes to personal and political revolution.

Especially when relating to the natural world, Andrée insisted that we think things through beyond our own personal convenience or inconvenience and she practised this in her daily life. For example, digging in the garden was not simply the turning over of soil for Andrée. Whenever she uncovered earthworms she would pick up each one and relocate it under mulch in another part of the garden or in the cool, sheltered earth and grass at the base of a bush. No matter how much longer it took her to turn the garden this way, Andrée safely replaced each worm. In winter, she put no log in the wood stove without first carefully inspecting it for any little life that might be seeking refuge in it. And then she would take that life to where it had the best chance of survival – indoors or out. Even when Andrée was seriously ill, her first impulse and action were to assist and protect the natural life around her. One summer day we were returning from the mechanic's shop in separate cars. Andrée, a distance ahead of me, stopped on the shore road to aid a turtle in her passage across the road from dry land to the bogs. I could hardly believe my eyes as I sped past this bent-over figure inching along the road behind a turtle and then suddenly realised – that's Andrée!

Andrée also recognised fixation on pain as a pitfall that prevents growth, movement, passion, joy. She saw that pain is so pervasive an experience for women in this culture and so expected by and for us as our daily fare that we can easily 'plug into' it. Correspondingly, it is too often easier for a woman to identify with another woman's pain than with her joy. Andrée always refused the role of victim by vigorously seeking ways to come through the difficult times, to turn circumstances around to her advantage. When all else failed, she waited out the storm with resilience and an indefatigable belief in life.

Andrée believed in the power of women as deeply as she believed in the power of nature: power to grow, to endure, to regenerate despite seeming losses. Her vision of women coming into knowledge of Self was inextricably bound up with women recognising, respecting, and participating in our common life with nature. And even if our wave did not have the force to reach shore now, she believed there were always enough women who with courage and determination would continue to name and act in harmony with this kinship.

Eventually Andrée moved to a plot of land in Norwell, Massachusetts which we tended and made a sanctuary for birds and squirrels, worms and bees, weeds and brambles. And it in turn was a sanctuary for ourselves where we sought refuge from the all-too-necessary jobs, where we could be free to work and write. Here, on a day-to-day basis, we slowly moved toward greater and greater self-sufficiency. This meant a lot of hard work but also a lot of fun, frustration as well as success. It is not easy to live responsibly with nature. It requires an ever-expanding consciousness and sensitivity to the variety of life forms; the willingness to understand and respond to that life; the wisdom to know when to let alone, to help along, or to discourage.

In creating this revolutionary life, Andrée drew upon her long intimacy with and caring for nature. These are no simple guides, and many painful dilemmas ensued. For example, we allowed the lovely but invasive wild roses to grow throughout the grape arbor, which often made harvesting grapes an exercise in self-mutilation. Or again, Andrée believed that to feed birds responsibly (and birds needed to be assisted because of massive habitat destruction and chem-lawns) the cats had to be kept indoors, a proposition clearly distressing to the cats. The shaky compromise was walks on a leash and/or supervised 'sessions' in the fenced-in garden.

In Norwell, Andrée was able to actualise some of the dreams of her childhood. She took deep pleasure in the gratuitous beauty of the world she created and the world she allowed to spontaneously be around her: the bittersweet creeping through the lilac, the iridescent sheen of the turkey's feathers when they caught the sun, the hens' familiar ways with her, the last scarlet blossom poised on the pinnacle of the bean vine. She derived immense satisfaction from projects she had never before attempted – roofing the garage, shingling the chicken coop, designing and building a wood shed with recycled lumber, rescuing a swarm of bees clustered at the top of a tall cedar tree. On the whole, she was happy and content. She was at peace and harmony with herself and the living world.

However, Andrée was never at peace with the patriarchal world. In fact, she was sorely tormented when confronted with the stupid, selfish destruction of nature and her creatures that is endemic to patriarchy. She was moved by a sense of acute urgency to *do something* about it. *Rape of the Wild* came to fruition in this blend of peace and discord, hope and despair. This book was Andrée's passionate effort to turn around as many minds and hearts as she could from the violation of nature towards awareness and responsible living.

Andrée died of cancer before her book was published and before we had completed many of the projects which were dear to her heart, like the rose garden. None the less, in her words and her work she has left us a rich legacy of courage and beauty, of strength and gentleness, of love and rage. Like her Foresisters who tasted deeply of life, Andrée has become a power of the universe. She is now, as she has always been, one with the earth and her elements.

Joyce Contrucci

Index